Advanced Introduction to Insurance Law

Elgar Advanced Introductions are stimulating and thoughtful introductions to major fields in the social sciences, business and law, expertly written by the world's leading scholars. Designed to be accessible yet rigorous, they offer concise and lucid surveys of the substantive and policy issues associated with discrete subject areas.

The aims of the series are two-fold: to pinpoint essential principles of a particular field, and to offer insights that stimulate critical thinking. By distilling the vast and often technical corpus of information on the subject into a concise and meaningful form, the books serve as accessible introductions for undergraduate and graduate students coming to the subject for the first time. Importantly, they also develop well-informed, nuanced critiques of the field that will challenge and extend the understanding of advanced students, scholars and policy-makers.

For a full list of titles in the series please see the back of the book. Recent titles in the series include:

Radical Innovation
Joe Tidd

Pricing Strategy and Analytics
Vithala R. Rao

Bounded Rationality
Clement A. Tisdell

International Food Law
Neal D. Fortin

International Conflict and Security Law
Second Edition
Nigel D. White

Entrepreneurial Finance
Second Edition
Hans Landström

US Civil Liberties
Susan N. Herman

Resilience
Fikret Berkes

Insurance Law
Robert H. Jerry, II

Advanced Introduction to

Insurance Law

ROBERT H. JERRY, II

Floyd R. Gibson Missouri Endowed Professor of Law Emeritus, School of Law, University of Missouri, and Dean Emeritus and Levin Mabie & Levin Professor of Law Emeritus, Levin College of Law, University of Florida, USA

Elgar Advanced Introductions

Edward Elgar
PUBLISHING

Cheltenham, UK • Northampton, MA, USA

Published by
Edward Elgar Publishing Limited
The Lypiatts
15 Lansdown Road
Cheltenham
Glos GL50 2JA
UK

Edward Elgar Publishing, Inc.
William Pratt House
9 Dewey Court
Northampton
Massachusetts 01060
USA

A catalogue record for this book
is available from the British Library

Library of Congress Control Number: 2023930846

This book is available electronically on Elgar Advanced Introductions: Law
www.advancedintros.com

Printed on elemental chlorine free (ECF)
recycled paper containing 30% Post-Consumer Waste

ISBN 978 1 80088 421 2 (cased)
ISBN 978 1 80088 422 9 (eBook)
ISBN 978 1 80088 423 6 (paperback)

Printed and bound in the USA

Contents

Preface

To convince someone that insurance is important, simply ask them to identify an event or transaction that does not involve insurance in some way. This is not easy to do. They may offer the example of a crime, but if we look closely enough, the odds are high that insurance is implicated in some manner. In civil affairs, it is nearly impossible to find an example. If insurance is so pervasive in our economic and social lives, the legal rules governing the industry are unquestionably worthy of our attention.

I appreciate the opportunity Edward Elgar Publishing has given me to articulate, after my nearly forty years of academic study and teaching, what thoughts I would share with someone interested in a more challenging and advanced introduction to the field of insurance law. This book is my effort to do that. Understanding insurance law presupposes some understanding of risk, how it is managed, and the insurance business, including how insurers interact with the consuming public. My discussion covers those topics and then addresses what I consider to be the principal themes of insurance law regulating those interactions. Because insurance law is so vast, sometimes in the discussion I offer representative examples of the issues insurance law addresses and leave it to the reader to seek more expansive texts, treatises, and articles for a deeper dive into the material. Some suggestions are provided in the footnotes.

As the co-author of a 975-page introductory treatise on insurance law, which I first wrote and published in 1987, I am grateful to Carolina Academic Press for supporting my desire to write this volume for Elgar. The treatise, now in its sixth edition with Douglas R. Richmond as co-author and last published in 2018, is titled *Understanding Insurance Law*. Its first citation appears in Chapter 2; thereafter, it appears in the footnotes as "JERRY AND RICHMOND." Readers should know that all

Internet sources cited in the footnotes were visited during the month of August 2022. Also, each chapter restarts the numbering at "1," and *supra* references are used only if the source appeared earlier in the chapter.

Last but hardly least, I want to acknowledge four of the "senior scholars" in insurance law whose early works influenced me greatly—Edwin Patterson, Robert Keeton, William Vance, and Spencer Kimball. I am grateful for my many years of co-authorship and collaboration with Roger Henderson and Doug Richmond. I also acknowledge with profound gratitude the benefits and insights I have received from the works of my contemporaries and an amazing cohort of young insurance scholars around the globe. You are too numerous to list here, but you are very much appreciated, and I look forward to reading your contributions for, I hope, many years to come.

Robert H. Jerry, II
Gainesville, Florida

1 Introduction to insurance law

The idea of risk is as old as human thought. Our earliest ancestors heard rustles in the grass and evaluated whether the noise was a dangerous lion or a harmless rabbit. Survival depended on correctly assessing the risk and choosing (and executing) an effective risk management strategy (most likely retreating until the facts were better understood). In our earliest organized societies, our ancestors understood mortality and recognized the costs associated with death. They formed groups based on mutual promises to bury their members and in some instances share the burdens of supporting survivors. When specialization led to a class of merchants who traded with their counterparts in other locales by traveling with their goods across seas and oceans, they adopted risk-spreading conventions to protect themselves and each other from the perils of the sea.

Eventually, some investors saw an opportunity to make a profit by assuming risk for a fee, betting on loss not occurring and the fee becoming their gain. A few hundred years later, recognizable markets existed where those with risks of loss could meet owners of capital and pay them to assume their risks. As wealth grew and economies became more complex, more intricate facilities emerged to enable these exchanges, and eventually corporate structures were created for the purpose of conducting the business of risk assumption.

Today, the business of insurance has matured into one of the largest, most important, and most recognizable businesses on the planet. Global insurance premiums in 2021 amounted to USD 6.9 trillion, which represented 7.0 percent of global GDP.[1] Beyond serving its stabilizing risk manage-

---

1 Swiss Re Institute, *Sigma*, No. 4 (2022), pp. 2, 35, https://www.swissre.com/institute/research/sigma-research/World-insurance-series.html.

ment role for firms and individuals, insurance companies and related agencies employ millions of people, are among the largest investors in financial markets, and constitute a major source of capital for economic growth.[2]

The law that regulates this immense and important industry has two major divisions.[3] One focuses on regulating the various entities that conduct insurance activities. The sources of these governing rules are primarily statutes and administrative regulations promulgated by national and local legislatures and agencies operating with delegated authority, although courts frequently become involved in resolving questions that arise when these laws are applied. The other major division is a set of judicially articulated principles that regulate the relationship between insurance company and policyholder. These rules are predominantly specialized applications of contract law, although tort law, agency law, and sometimes statutes and administrative regulations are relevant.

Inevitably, insurance law, because the industry it regulates is so large and important, has far-ranging scope and a seemingly limitless array of details. Thus, this book, which is designed to be read in its entirety in a couple of hours, is necessarily an introduction to insurance law—but an introduction for the reader who wants a sense of not only the governing principles and rules but also the policies, values, and purposes that shape them. Thus, this advanced introduction seeks to preserve the value of brevity while engaging the complexities that come with peeling back the veneer and examining what lies underneath. Accordingly, this book can serve as the first stop for someone preparing for a deeper course of study, or it can be the last stop for someone who simply wants to satisfy a curi-

---

2 *See*, e.g., Liyan Han et al., *Insurance Development and Economic Growth*, 35 The Geneva Papers 183 (2010), https://doi.org/10.1057/gpp.2010.4 (discussing data from 77 developed and developing economies); Eur. Cent. Bank, *Financial Stability Review* (Dec. 2009), pp. 160–169, https://www.ecb.europa.eu/pub/financial-stability/fsr/html/all_releases.en.html (discussing role of insurers as market investors); Ins. Infor. Inst., *Employment in Insurance 2012921*, https://www.iii.org/fact-statistic/facts-statistics-industry-overview#Employment%20In%20Insurance,%202012-2021 (reporting that in 2021, the number of people employed by insurance entities in the US was 2.8 million, or almost 2 percent of the entire US labor force).

3 *See* Robert H. Jerry, II, *Insurance*, in The Oxford Companion to American Law (Kermit L. Hall et al., eds.), pp. 420–423 (2002).

osity about why insurance—both the business and the law that governs it—is so incredibly important.

To these ends, the discussion proceeds as follows. Chapter 2 examines the roles and meaning of insurance, placing insurance in the context of the broader goals of risk management. Chapter 3 explores different conceptions of insurance, explaining that, although usually framed as a particular kind of contract, insurance can also be understood as product, public utility, or a form of governance. Chapter 4 provides an overview of the insurance business, and Chapter 5 explains the basic contours of insurance law and regulation in more detail than this introduction. Chapter 6 explains the elements of the typical insurance policy and their significance within the legal frame of contract.

Chapter 7 explores the fundamental assumptions of insurance (fortuity, insurable interest, and indemnity) and the legal rules emanating from these assumptions. Chapter 8 returns to the historical conception of insurance as contract and examines the influence of contract law on modern insurance law. Chapter 9 takes up some representative issues that define the scope of common insurance coverages. Chapter 10 focuses on liability insurance, a common and important type of coverage that raises unique issues not confronted in other product lines.

Finally, Chapter 11 finishes the discussion by returning to the question "why insurance matters" and examining some current issues in insurance law and regulation. The topics discussed in this chapter connect to important questions of public policy, where insurance will play a significant role in shaping the characteristics of the future world in which we and future generations will live.

2 The purpose, meaning, and roles of insurance

2.1 Risk: its nature and strategies for managing it

2.1.1 The inevitability of risk

A fascinating way to narrate the story of human history involves explaining how humans have responded to risk through the millennia, i.e., by recognizing it, conceptualizing it, and then managing it.[1] Humanity's affinity for some risk-taking is almost certainly inherent in our species because every civilization with a recorded history is known to have had a thriving culture of gambling—i.e., betting and games of chance. In fact, the first serious effort to undertake a statistical analysis of probability occurred in the 1500s when Cardano, an Italian intellectual who happened to be a gambling addict, searched for ways to improve his chances of making successful wagers. What Cardano and some of his contemporaries realized was that these games, and some other questions involving uncertainty, were anchored in probabilities rather than pure randomness. It was not until the 1600s that a group of mathematicians, philosophers, and scientists—including such luminaries as Huygens, Pascal, Méré, Graunt, and Fermat (a lawyer for whom mathematics was a diversion!)—engaged in the first systematic efforts to articulate a theory of probability, which laid the foundations for later efforts to explain and quantify risk.

What motivated most of these early studies of chance was an appreciation that risk is more than an aspect of games humans play; it is a fundamental

---

1 For more discussion on the history of risk and efforts to manage it, *see* PETER L. BERNSTEIN, AGAINST THE GODS: THE REMARKABLE STORY OF RISK (1996).

element of the human condition. Risk is, and has always been, encompassed in every aspect of the lives of all creatures with enough brainpower to evaluate and make choices among alternative futures. When our earliest ancestors left their shelters and heard a rustling in the bush, judgments had to be made as to whether the noise was likely a squirrel hustling to its nest or a tiger looking for a meal. Those who exercised caution when encountering this risk were more likely to survive this encounter than those who did not, and patterns of alertness and reaction were ultimately baked into our species' DNA—one of the earliest examples of risk management in action. Indeed, when one surveys the way thinking animals interact with their environment and each other, and the way they evaluate circumstances, make judgments, and act on them, it is apparent that evolution has hard-wired many of these assessments into automatic reactions buried in living creatures' subconscious thought.

The overarching reality for these observations is that the world is an uncertain place. Events are not completely random, but few events are absolutely certain. Even events that are certain to occur at some point—such as death, to take an obvious example—are uncertain as to their timing. We can be certain that accidents will occur, but how many, when, and where is quite uncertain. We know that natural disasters will occur, but their timing, frequency, and intensity are uncertain. The undeniable overarching truth confronting every human being, whether we are referring to events outside our control or those triggered and directed by human agency, is that life is uncertain.

2.1.2 Quantifying risk

The inherent uncertainty of events can be described in terms of chance or probability. In insurance and many other contexts, we say that there is a *risk* that something might occur in the future—or might not. The possible occurrence might be something beneficial (like winning the lottery) or something harmful (like one's house being destroyed), so risks can be *positive* or *negative*. We often quantify risk by referring to specific probabilities that something might happen, such as when we say, for example, that a 75-year-old woman has a 2.4 percent chance of dying within the next 12 months.[2] It is also common to quantify risk by multiplying the

2 This is the 2019 figure, as reported in 2022, for the "Social Security population" in the US, which consists of US residents (states and territories) and

risk of exposure (i.e., the probability that something will happen) by the amount of impact (i.e., the magnitude of loss should the event occur). High-impact events that are highly probable to occur are the most important to manage, whereas low-impact events that rarely occur are the least important—and infinite combinations exist between these two extremes.

Also, in the insurance business, the term "risk" is sometimes used to refer to perils. For example, we might say that wind, fire, freezing, hail, crop failure, business interruption, etc. are the "risks" we seek to manage or to which an insurance contract applies. The common denominator for all these perils is that from the perspective of the risk manager or the insurance policyholder, these perils (and the amount of loss they will produce) are uncertain in their occurrence.

People make judgments about risk constantly. Before engaging in any activity, a person makes a judgment about costs and benefits, and the likelihood (or probability) that these costs or benefits will materialize. Sometimes the calculation is automatic, even subconscious; at other times, it involves a deliberate evaluation of available facts and assumptions. For example, when one evaluates whether to walk across a street at a corner where there is a stoplight as opposed to crossing the street in the middle of a block, one assesses the safety of these options (the risk of loss) against the benefit (time saved) by crossing in the middle of the block, the less safe option. Ideally, this calculation is neutral, objective, and rational, and is based on a complete understanding of all relevant information. The reality, however, is that preconceptions based on individual experience, emotion, intuition, fear, and psychology are typically wrapped up in this calculation, not to mention information gaps that impede the estimate. This mix of factors tends to cause inaccurate—sometimes wildly inaccurate—calculations about risk. This explains why some people who are afraid to fly in airplanes, which is extremely safe by all objective measures, do not think twice about driving an automobile after consuming two or three alcoholic beverages. It explains why people ignore obvious, abstract risks that can be alleviated easily (such as, for example, using sunscreen at the beach to alleviate the risk of skin cancer) but fret about things that are highly unlikely (such as, for example, being

US citizens living abroad. The equivalent figure for a 75-year-old man is 3.46 percent. Office of the Chief Actuary, Social Security. Admin., *Actuarial Life Table* (undated), https://www.ssa.gov/oact/STATS/table4c6.html.

attacked by a shark while in the water). Easily imaginable, horrific risks (e.g., terrorism attacks, home invasions, plane crashes) are among the least likely events to be evaluated objectively. Many other heuristics skew how humans evaluate risk.[3]

At some point, however, a calculation about probability, costs, and benefits will be made, and a choice to proceed with an activity—or not—will happen. At this point, a person will decide whether—and, if so, how—to manage the perceived risk of the decision.

2.1.3 Methods of managing risk

Risk management can occur in several ways.[4] First, we might manage risk by *minimizing the probability of negative outcomes* through efforts to prevent losses from occurring. For example, adding an automatic braking system to an automobile, so that the car will stop on its own before colliding with a pedestrian, object, or other vehicle prevents accidents from occurring (along with the associated deaths, injuries, and property damage). Second, we might manage risk by *minimizing the consequences of events* that occur. For example, installing air bags in automobiles and setting anti-crush requirements for their passenger compartments will not prevent accidents from occurring, but these loss-mitigation efforts will reduce the deaths and injuries that occur when accidents happen.

Accident prevention and loss minimization are two of the most important risk management strategies, but there are others. When choosing and combining multiple alternatives is an option and when the probabilities of these individual alternatives generating loss vary, *diversification* becomes possible and can serve as a powerful tool for managing risk. Diversification works because the risk of loss associated with relying on a single alternative is offset by simultaneously relying on other alternatives. It is unlikely that all alternatives will fail simultaneously; thus, if one alternative fails, losses will be mitigated when the other alternatives

---

3 For more discussion of the psychology of risk assessment, see Christopher Chabris & Daniel Simons, The Invisible Gorilla and Other Ways Our Intuitions Deceive Us (2011); Gerd Gigerenzer, Calculated Risks: How to Know When Numbers Deceive You (2002).

4 *See* Robert H. Jerry, II & Douglas R. Richmond, Understanding Insurance Law, pp. 9–11 (6th ed. 2018) (hereafter "Jerry & Richmond").

continue to perform. Having more alternatives in play makes it more likely that at least one alternative will fail, but the maximation of gains is sacrificed to a small extent to reduce the probability of a catastrophic loss of all gains. The most obvious illustration of diversification in action is an investor's creation of a diverse portfolio that spreads the risks of gains and losses over a large number of stocks, bonds, and other investment vehicles, but diversification manages risk in any situation where multiple alternatives functioning independently of each other can be selected and deployed simultaneously.

When risk cannot be managed through prevention, mitigation, or diversification, one might choose to *self-insure* the risk. This strategy usually involves creating a reserve through which future losses are paid or covered; if a loss occurs, the reserve is replenished. A good way to understand this strategy is imagining someone committing to pay the equivalent of an insurance premium to oneself to create a reserve; if the reserve is fully funded and no loss occurs, the payment of the next recurring premium is excused. The self-insurance strategy essentially involves a choice to bear the risk out of one's own assets. People or firms with great wealth or assets are most likely to self-insure, but it is extremely common for anyone seeking to manage a risk to self-insure a portion of a risk as a part of an overall risk management strategy.

Whenever one faces a risk management choice, one might opt to ignore the question and do nothing, or to procrastinate by putting off the decision. Doing nothing, however, is a choice; it is an implicit rejection of all proactive risk management alternatives. Procrastination is simply a decision to do nothing for the time being, but doing nothing is a risk management strategy because it is essentially a decision to self-insure the risk.

The extent to which an individual or firm opts for one or more of these strategies depends on their comfort level about risk. This will be shaped by multiple factors, including the probability and potential magnitude of loss, one's ability to absorb a loss, and the extent of one's psychological and emotional tolerance for insecurity. When confronting a risk of loss, people are either risk-preferring, risk-neutral, or risk-averse. Imagine being forced to choose between a 50 percent chance of losing $10,000 (which is an *expected loss* of $5,000) or the certainty of losing $5,000. A risk-preferring person would choose the 50/50 "coin-flip" option (an equal probability of losing either $10,000 or nothing) to the certainty of losing $5,000. For the risk-preferring person, a 50 percent chance of losing $10,000 is preferable to a certain loss of $5,000. In contrast, a risk-averse person prefers a certain loss of $5,000 to avoid the 50 percent chance of losing $10,000. Risk-neutral persons are indifferent to the alternatives. As the adverse impacts from potential losses increase, risk-aversion tends to increase. Thus, a person who is risk-neutral in the foregoing example is likely to become more risk-averse if the loss is something that would be devastating if it occurred (such as the loss of one's home or business). By the same logic, the more wealth a person has, the less risk-averse they become. This is because a wealthy person is more likely to be indifferent about risks that are of far greater concern to a person with less financial capacity.

2.1.4 Insurance: the strategy of last resort for the risk-averse

If a person is averse to a risk and the strategies of prevention, loss mitigation, diversification, and self-insurance do not address it satisfactorily, the remaining strategy is *transferring the risk* to someone else. As economies have evolved, markets have emerged in which some persons are willing to assume risk if they are paid to take it on. This is not a situation where risk-preferring persons make deals with risk-averse persons. Rather, it is a market where firms, which are also risk-averse, assume the risks of many similarly situated persons and then use *the law of large numbers* to distribute the risk across the entire pool of risk-transferring persons, which has the effect of eliminating the risk.[5]

How does this remarkable result happen? The law of large numbers is a statistical principle which holds that as the number of observed events in a sample increases, the more the difference between the observed value of the sample and its true value declines. To illustrate, imagine two merchants (whose risks are independent of each other), each of whom has a 20 percent chance of losing $100,000 and an 80 percent chance of losing nothing (a 20 percent chance of losing $100,000 is an expected loss of $20,000). If these merchants decide to pool their gains and losses, each merchant's risk of losing the full $20,000 declines from 20 percent to 4 percent; the risk of losing nothing drops from 80 percent to 64 percent; and there is a 32 percent chance of losing $10,000, which reflects the prob-

---

5 *See* JERRY & RICHMOND, pp. 12–15.

ability that one merchant will lose everything and the other nothing.[6] For the risk-averse merchant, this is a good arrangement, because the risk of losing everything declines from 20 percent to 4 percent.[7] If a few thousand other merchants can be persuaded to join this deal, the odds that each merchant will avoid a catastrophic loss and retain between $78,000 and $82,000 rises to 99.9 percent, essentially converting a 20 percent chance of a massive loss into a virtual certainty that a catastrophic loss will not occur. The merchant is also virtually certain to lose $20,000 (recall that this was the value of the expected loss), but this is the price of being freed from the risk of suffering a $100,000 loss. The beauty of this arrangement is that it enables the merchant to plan a future. Without the ability to avoid the risk of a catastrophic loss, many of these merchants would not enter the business in the first place, as the high risk of catastrophic failure would suffocate their entrepreneurial spirit. A risk-averse person, when faced with a one-in-five chance of losing $100,000, would prefer the certain loss of $20,000—and would be willing to pay an amount larger than that in exchange for eliminating the possibility of a catastrophic loss.

The arrangement just described is the essence of insurance. The insurance company facilitates risk-averse persons (i.e., policyholders) paying the insurer to accept a transfer of the risk, and the insurer's ability to make the same contract with thousands of other similarly situated persons enables the insurer to use the law of large numbers to predict with near certainty how many losses will be suffered in the pool during a specified interval of time. That knowledge allows the insurer to charge the policyholders a sufficient premium to cover the predicted losses and the insurer's overhead in administering the pooling mechanism, plus a profit (if the insurer is a for-profit enterprise). This market exists because policyholders are typically willing to pay an insurer more than the expected loss in exchange

---

6 The math underlying this result is as follows: If two merchants each have a 1-in-5 chance of a loss, the chances that both will simultaneously suffer a loss, which is calculated by multiplying the two probabilities together, is 1-in-25 (or 4 percent). Each merchant's risk of losing nothing is 4-in-5 (or 80 percent), but if they pool their gains and losses, the risk that both merchants will lose nothing is 16-in-25, or 64 percent. The probability that one merchant will have a loss while the other does not is the remainder, i.e., 8-in-25, or 32 percent.

7 The risk of losing nothing declines from 80 percent to 64 percent, but the higher risk of a partial loss is better for a risk-averse merchant if the risk of a total loss declines dramatically.

for the insurer accepting a transfer of the risk. The difference between the premium paid and the expected loss represents the value the policyholder places on eliminating the insecurity that accompanies the risk.

This last observation reveals another key point about the nature of an insurance contract. An insurance contract is not a mere wager or bet with the insurer about whether a particular event (and accompanying loss) will happen during the policy term. Rather, what the policyholder buys is the elimination of the stress, anxiety, and insecurity that accompanies vulnerability to a risk of loss. This elimination of insecurity has present value; it occurs at the moment the policy becomes effective—and the policyholder receives this benefit even if a loss is not suffered during the policy term.

Three caveats are important. First, the law of large numbers works only if the risks assembled in the pool are independent of each other, i.e., the risks must not be *correlated*. To illustrate, if a single event would cause everyone, or substantially everyone, in the pool to suffer a loss simultaneously, the risk is not distributed throughout the pool. To use the example above, a one-in-five chance of an event occurring that will cause all merchants in the pool to suffer a loss simultaneously does not distribute risk, but instead simply transfers the 20 percent chance of total loss to the insurer. Insurers are also risk-averse, and they will not insure a correlated risk unless they can transfer it to someone else (which is sometimes possible in reinsurance markets, where insurers essentially buy insurance from other insurers called *reinsurers*).

Second, the description above assumes that all members of the pool have identical risk profiles, but this is only possible in theory. No matter how successful an insurer may be in assembling a pool of similarly situated insureds, differences will exist among members of the pool, and some of these differences will be relevant to how the risk being insured should be priced. Moreover, those who have information about their risk profiles and know that they are at greater risk for loss are more likely to seek insurance. Insurers will seek to identify those who have higher risks and charge them a higher premium, but at a certain point the cost of discovering information about insureds becomes too high to justify the search. This means that some insureds will know more about their risks than insurers do, and these information asymmetries inevitably result in insurance pools being composed of a disproportionate number of higher-risk insureds. This principle is called *adverse selection*. Many insurance company practices are intended, and some insurance law rules can be understood, as efforts to combat adverse selection.

The point, then, is that some insureds in pools created by insurers are more similar than others. Insurers strive to identify the dissimilarities, and if lower-risk insureds can be identified and it is cost-effective to offer these insureds a lower premium (i.e., if the costs of identifying and reliably measuring distinctions among insureds do not outweigh the benefits that can be gained by charging low-risk insureds a lower premium, and, ergo, higher-risk insureds a higher premium), the pool will be divided based on the identified distinction. Even though these subdivided pools will have their risks more accurately priced, each of these pools will be subject to the same adverse selection principle that operated in the original pool, and insurers will continue to subdivide pools if it is cost-effective to do so. Notably, insurers have strong incentives to try to identify better tools for pricing risk and classifying insureds. If an insurer finds a way to effectively subdivide risk pools before its competitors do, that insurer will be able to assemble a new, lower-priced pool which has the potential to lure low-risk insureds eligible for this superiorly priced product from the insurer's competitors, leaving the competitors with a higher-risk, higher-priced, and ultimately less profitable pool. To summarize, "similarly situated" is a relative term, with the degree of similarity depending on the interaction of complex market forces.

Third, once individuals have insurance, a tendency exists for policyholders to take fewer precautions to prevent loss—which means that the purchase of insurance has the perverse effect of increasing loss. To illustrate, if the owner of a smartphone does not insure it for theft and accidental breakage, the owner will be more likely to secure it when not using it and take greater care not to drop it. But if the smartphone is insured, the owner will be less likely to take these precautions when it is inconvenient to do so. The transaction costs of dealing with loss will still encourage the owner to be careful, but at the margin, the existence of insurance makes it slightly more likely that a loss will occur. This economic principle is called *moral hazard*. Moral hazard exists in other settings, but its effect in insurance is manifested in insurance's tendency to attract persons who intend to cause loss (and believe they can escape detection), to cause some insureds in economic distress to trigger loss for their own economic benefit (i.e., to convert an asset to cash—if they believe they can escape detection), and to cause some insureds to take fewer precautions, thereby increasing the number of loss-producing occurrences. As with adverse selection, many insurance company practices and some insurance law rules can be understood as efforts to combat moral hazard.

2.2 Why insurance matters

Purchasing insurance is the risk management strategy of last resort, but it is an extremely important last resort. Indeed, the domestic and global economies and social order as we presently know them would not exist in the absence of insurance.

First, insurance plays a vital role in promoting economic activity. Take, for example, an individual or firm contemplating the creation of a new business enterprise which, if it succeeds, would create many jobs, new income and wealth, new spending, and through the multiplier effect more businesses of all kinds and descriptions. But the start-up costs for this new enterprise are massive, and a risk exists that the enterprise might fail due to an occurrence outside their control (imagine a fire or other disaster destroying the manufacturing plant). This occurrence would be a bankrupting event with catastrophic, long-term financial implications for the owners. In the absence of a risk transfer and distribution mechanism, the individual or firm may well choose to forego creating the business rather than confront the risk of suffering a bankrupting loss with highly adverse consequences. But if this risk and all the insecurity it entails can be replaced with a steady, certain stream of payments made in exchange for a third party's agreement to assume that risk, the individual or firm can then place a line item in the annual budget that represents the cost of achieving security and eliminating the risk of loss. The enterprise can plan for this recurring, predictable expense and proceed accordingly. When one realizes that this narrative plays out repeatedly in businesses of all kinds, it becomes apparent that insurance is indispensable to commercial activity and economic growth.

Second, a variation of the foregoing narrative also plays out in the non-commercial world with equivalent importance but slightly different implications. As civilizations matured and economies grew, wealth expanded and individuals became more affluent, which also meant that more situations existed where people could suffer loss. With affluence came more risk, but affluence also created the wherewithal to invest in arrangements that transfer and spread these emergent risks. For individuals and families, the loss of a home, the death or disability of someone whose income sustains a family, or the levy of a crushing judgment because of an act of negligence that injures another are all examples of catastrophic events with potentially multi-generational adverse consequences. In short, it is impossible to imagine our personal lives being organized as they are today in the absence of the ability to enter into insurance arrangements that protect individual and family wealth and facilitate inter-generational transfers of assets. The security provided by these insurance arrangements cannot be understated.

What happens when insurance fails? In other words, what happens when insurance is unavailable and cannot be purchased for a particular risk? What happens when an insurance company becomes insolvent? The preliminary question is whether the risk in question is one that is worth transferring and distributing, or whether it is one that should be left on the party who bears it. This question will be asked and answered in the political process, where a decision will be made as to whether the tools of government should be used to spread the risk across all members of society. Nobel Prize-winning economist Kenneth Arrow explained that non-existent or underdeveloped markets for risk constitute one of the largest failings of free-market economies,[8] and that it is government's role to "undertake insurance in those cases where this [private insurance] market, for whatever reason, has failed to emerge."[9] In other words, government—if it chooses to act—is actually the insurer of last resort,[10] and, to be strictly accurate, asking government to insure the risk is technically the strategy of last resort.

---

8 *See* Kenneth J. Arrow & Robert C. Lind, *Uncertainty and the Evaluation of Public Investment Decisions*, 60 Am. Econ. Rev. 374 (1970).

9 Kenneth J. Arrow, *Uncertainty and the Welfare Economics of Medical Care*, 53 Am. Econ. Rev. 941, 961 (1963).

10 Risk management is not generally considered to be a government function, but the reality is that much of what government does reduces or allocates risk. Bankruptcy law, product liability law, workplace safety rules, banking and financial regulations, and corporate law generally (with its limited liability rules), to name a few, are all important risk management systems. For more discussion, *see* David A. Moss, When All Else Fails: Government as the Ultimate Risk Manager (2002).

2.3 Defining insurance

Imagining a transaction that does not involve transfer or allocation of risk is difficult, as that is essentially what contracts do when they create expectations. Take, for example, a loan of money by a creditor to a debtor, to be repaid with interest. Unless reallocated, the creditor bears the risk of the debtor's default, but this risk is usually shifted by the creditor taking a security interest in property owned by the debtor. This transfers the risk to the debtor, whose property will be seized as payment of the debt if the debtor defaults. Alternatively, the creditor may insist that the debtor have a guarantor who promises to pay the debt if the debtor defaults; this shifts the risk of the default from the creditor to the guarantor.

Simple contracts of sale allocate risk; even price-setting itself is an allocation of risk. Assume a farmer contracts today to sell a harvest to a buyer with delivery to occur at a specified future date. If the agreement is to sell at the market price on the delivery date, the farmer assumes the risk that prices might fall between now and the delivery date (and the buyer assumes the risk that prices might rise). If the parties agree to set the price for future delivery at today's market price, the buyer assumes the risk of price declines, and the farmer assumes the risk of price increases. To take another example, conditions are powerful risk allocation provisions, and most contracts contain them. Assume a buyer desires to purchase a seller's house, but the buyer, lacking enough cash to pay the price, needs a loan to make the purchase. If seller and buyer reach an unconditional agreement for the sale of the house, the buyer bears the risk of not getting the loan—and if the buyer is unable to secure the loan, the buyer's inability to perform the contract will constitute a breach and they will be liable for damages. But the buyer can shift this risk to the seller if the parties agree upon a condition that the buyer need not proceed with the purchase if the buyer is unable to secure a loan.

None of these examples involve insurance. All involve risk transfer and allocation, and some others to be discussed later also involve distribution, but this is not enough to turn them into insurance transactions. Insurance involves something more. Thus, a working definition of insurance is needed.

Stated most simply, *insurance is an arrangement for the transfer and distribution of risk.*[11] *Risk*, i.e., the uncertainty of loss, is the object of the arrangement. The security created by the arrangement, which happens when risk is reduced or eliminated, is essentially the product that the person purchasing insurance seeks to acquire. The *arrangement* is an agreement—i.e., a contract[12]—under which one party, the policyholder (the individual or firm that purchased and owns the policy; sometimes the policyholder is called the "insured," but someone can be insured under a policy and not be the purchaser and owner) pays the other (the insurance company) to take over the risk. *Transfer* refers to the shift of the risk from policyholder to insurance company, meaning that if the risk subsequently manifests itself in a loss, the insurer, which has assumed the risk, will bear the loss by reimbursing the policyholder for the losses suffered or will otherwise assume responsibility for the consequences of the risk's manifestation. *Distribution* refers to the fact that transfer of risk is not enough to create an insurance arrangement. What is essential to an insurance contract is that the insurance company create a pool of policyholders for the purpose of distributing the risk across the pool.

Yet sometimes the presence of agreement, transfer, and distribution is not enough to stake out the boundary between insurance and a non-insurance transaction. Some arrangements seem to function like insurance but are nevertheless generally understood not to constitute insurance.

---

11 Robert E. Keeton, Insurance Law, p. 2 (1971). Similar definitions have been offered by others. *See*, e.g., C.A. Kulp & John W. Hall, Casualty Insurance, p. 10 (4th ed. 1968) ("insurance is a formal social device for the substitution of certainty for uncertainty through the pooling of risks"); George E. Rejda & Michael J. McNamara, Principles of Risk Management and Insurance, p. 20 (12th ed. 2014) (defining insurance as an "arrangement" that includes "[p]ooling of losses[,] [p]ayment of fortuitous losses[,] [r]isk transfer[, and] [i]ndemnification"). For a more precise definition, *see* Jerry & Richmond, p. 16 ("A contract of insurance is an agreement in which one party (the insurer), in exchange for a consideration (usually called a 'premium') provided by the other party (the policyholder), assumes the other party's risk and distributes it across a group of similarly situated persons, each of whose risk has been assumed in a similar transaction").

12 In contract law, an agreement exists when two or more persons express mutual assent to exchange something. Not all agreements are enforceable; if the agreement meets the requirements for enforceability, it is a contract.

Take the example of a product warranty: a seller sells a product to a buyer, warrants the quality of the product, and promises that if the product fails to operate as warranted, the seller will repair or replace the product at no charge to the buyer. From one perspective, this agreement looks like the seller is providing the buyer with insurance against product failure. The risk the buyer bears of such failure is transferred back to the seller; the seller's payment to fulfill the repair or replace obligation comes from a reserve created by an additional charge (resembling a premium) levied as part of the purchase price upon all buyers. Indeed, the law of large numbers is operating here; the manufacturer who creates and sells a large number of products makes an informed prediction that some of its products will fail to perform as expected, and adjusts the price charged accordingly. In other words, product warranties have characteristics of transfer (the risk of failure of the product is shifted from the product's owner back to the manufacturer) and distribution (the manufacturer creates a reserve to pay losses from payments made by buyers), but no one seriously contends that all manufacturers and sellers who create warranties are conducting the business of insurance. The correct analysis is that the primary object and purpose of a contract for sale of a product is exactly that—the sale of the product—and not the purchase of security that the product will be replaced if it fails. The risk transfer and distribution features of the deal are at the periphery of the transaction and are not the buyer's main purpose when purchasing the product. In contrast, the primary object and purpose of an insurance contract is the transfer of risk itself, i.e., the insurer agreeing to assume an insured's risk as its own in exchange for the insured paying a premium to the insurer, and then distributing that risk in a pool of risks assumed in similar transactions.

This result is often explained by what is called the *principal object and purpose test*. When a warranty is created to accompany a sale of a product, the principal object and purpose of the contract is the sale of the product—not the creation of the warranty (where risk is, in fact, transferred and distributed). To constitute insurance, the transfer of *the risk itself* must be the principal object and purpose of the contract. In an insurance transaction, the buyer's primary and overriding purpose is not to buy a product or a thing, but is to buy *security*—the assurance that if a loss happens, the buyer will not suffer it, and the insurer will instead. This test, or some variation of it, is the core principle that distinguishes insurance contracts from arrangements that have a risk transfer and distribution effect but do not qualify as insurance contracts. Ultimately, what is at stake when this boundary is drawn is whether government officials charged with regulating the business of insurance have authority to regulate the transaction in question.

Under this test, the location of the boundary is not always obvious. For example, the warranty example above becomes more complex if the warranty is offered by a third-party who is not the original seller or manufacturer of the product. From one perspective, this kind of transaction looks more like insurance because protecting against the risk of product failure is the sole objective of the contract—even when this is offered as an extension of the original warranty, which is usually how many third-party warranties are sold. Yet if the warranty provider requires repairs to be done by agents of the provider, the transaction begins to look more like an exclusive dealing arrangement (i.e., a requirements contract), where the buyer promises to purchase all needed repair services from the warranty provider at discounted prices. If the extended warranty covers damages by collisions and other fortuitous events, then the arrangement is more likely to be deemed insurance. In some jurisdictions, statutes label these businesses as *warranty associations* and delegate the authority to regulate them to insurance departments.

Another example of a borderline transaction is the *collision damage waiver* (CDW) offered by most vehicle rental companies, and which is commonly described as "insurance" when it is presented to lessees as a supplemental option at the time of the rental. Because the lessee is told that accepting the offer protects the lessee from liability for damage to the vehicle, the lessee is likely to understand the product as insurance even if it is not labeled as such. Yet upon closer scrutiny, the transaction involves the lessor waiving its right under the law of bailment to insist that the property be returned to the lessor in the same condition as when it was leased, less ordinary wear and tear. The release of a right, if nothing more occurs, is not insurance; the principal object and purpose of the transaction is the waiver of a right in exchange for a payment. The rental company may pool, in a manner similar to what happens with a product warranty, the supplemental payments and use them in much the same way an insurance company creates and uses a reserve, but this does not change the fact that the primary purpose of the transaction is the lessor's waiver of a right recognized by the law of bailment.

The CDW example is challenging because the lessee is, in fact, purchasing security. Moreover, there may be good public policy reasons to regulate CDWs. Historically, vehicle rental companies have sold CDWs at prices per unit of coverage that greatly exceed what an insurance policy providing the same coverage would cost. Moreover, trade practices that pressure lessees to purchase CDWs are similar to the kinds of pressures that have led to the regulation of marketing practices in the insurance industry. In many jurisdictions, legislatures have enacted laws that regulate CDWs, thereby mooting the question of whether CDWs constitute insurance, and sometimes the authority to regulate CDWs has been given to the insurance regulators, no doubt because CDWs have some similarities to insurance contracts and insurance departments have the relevant expertise to serve as the governing agency.[13]

To summarize, whether a particular transaction constitutes insurance can be a difficult question, and not all judicial decisions where this question arises are consistent. At the question's core, the answer turns on whether the primary purpose of the transaction is to trade the uncertainty of risk for the security that comes with a promise that the transferor will be protected in the event the risk materializes in a loss, or whether the primary purpose of the transaction is something else. Sometimes a type of transaction that fits more neatly within the category of non-insurance arrangements is nevertheless deemed appropriate for government regulation for reasons like those which serve as the rationales for regulating insurance companies. This last observation underscores the ultimate significance of the legal rules that define insurance. Because insurance contracts are regulated by government agencies, the ultimate importance of the definition of insurance is delineating the limit of these agencies' authority, because non-insurance transactions, absent a specific delegation to regulate them, fall outside the scope of these agencies' oversight.

2.4 Roles of insurance beyond risk spreading

The importance of insurance as a risk transfer and distribution device often leads to other important roles of insurance being overlooked. This section discusses five roles of insurance beyond risk spreading: capital

---

13 For more discussion, see JERRY & RICHMOND, pp. 13–20.

accumulation and allocation; information production and dissemination; gatekeeping; redistribution of wealth; and reflecting and influencing social norms.[14]

Sometimes overlooked in discussions of the insurance business is the fact that insurance companies are enormous financial institutions that compete with banks and securities firms for the *accumulation of capital* and then serve as important *allocators of capital*. Insurers need large sums of capital to fund reserves that will be used to pay claims filed by insureds who suffer losses. The investment of these funds provides a critical source of revenue that supports insurers' income and solvency, but the larger point is that how these funds are invested has enormous implications for the functioning of domestic and global economies. Insurer investments are major forces in markets for stocks, bonds (both commercial and government), real estate, commercial loans, venture capital funds, and almost every other sector where a return can be earned on capital. Government regulations can steer insurance capital into market or industry sectors that policymakers want to support or grow. Thus, capital accumulation and allocation are major and important roles of insurance companies.

Because the business of insurance depends on accurate predictions of future losses, insurance companies invest heavily in acquiring, understanding, and effectively using information. In other words, insurers have a key role in society as *information producers and disseminators*. Obviously, it is important to insurers that they be able to identify the kinds of losses that may occur, choose which ones they wish to insure, predict the frequency and magnitude of events, and calculate the premiums to charge for covering the risks. But reducing claims, both in terms of the number of events and size of losses, reduces insurer expenses, and thus insurers often use their accumulated information to help policyholders prevent and mitigate losses. It is true that insurers treat much of the information they accumulate as proprietary, but major portions of the information they assemble are highly relevant to important issues of

---

14 For additional reading and discussion, *see* Tom Baker, Kyle D. Logue & Chaim Saiman, Insurance Law and Policy, pp. 6–26 (5th ed. 2021); Kenneth S. Abraham, Distributing Risk: Insurance, Legal Theory, and Public Policy (1986); Spencer L. Kimball, Insurance and Public Policy (1960); Omri Ben-Shahar & Kyle D. Logue, *How Insurance Substitutes for Regulation*, 36:1 Regulation 36 (2013).

local, national, and global concern, and are made available to inform and influence public policy choices.

Insurance plays an important *gatekeeping role* in many aspects of society. Some things that individuals and firms want to do require the prior purchase of insurance, which sometimes makes insurance companies a decision-maker on whether the transaction or activity will occur. For example, a home buyer who needs a loan to buy a house will not get the loan without purchasing homeowner's insurance protecting the creditor's interest in the property—and if no insurer will issue a policy, the purchase will not occur. Many jurisdictions do not require doctors to have medical malpractice insurance, but many hospitals will not extend privileges to physicians who lack it. One cannot lawfully own and operate a motor vehicle without liability insurance—and if one does so, sanctions are possible, such as suspension of a driver's license, vehicle impoundment, and fines and reinstatement fees. One who aspires to do these things must meet the insurance companies' standards, which makes private insurance companies an important regulator of activities and who gets to do them.

As discussed above, distribution of risk is an essential characteristic of insurance. Thus, it follows that insurance redistributes assets from those who purchase insurance and do not suffer losses to the unfortunate individuals within pools who do. Thus, insurance has *redistributive effects* on how assets and resources are allocated in a society. When individuals and firms voluntarily purchase insurance, they make a proactive choice to participate in this redistributive process, which reflects a shared value held by all within the pool that losses of the less fortunate should be borne by all who subscribe to the arrangement. When the purchase of insurance is compulsory, as it is with automobile liability insurance and in some countries with health insurance, this redistribution from the fortunate to the unfortunate is a mandatory redistribution, occasioned by the inability of market forces to cause these pools to be organized and the political judgment that their formation is essential to the public interest.

Redistributive effects, however, go beyond the simple transfer of assets from the fortunate to the unfortunate. The choice of factors used to price insurance (this is called *rating*) also have the effect of redistributing wealth from one or more sectors of society to other sectors. Sometimes government regulations require premiums to be set at actuarially unfair rates, meaning that the rates are not set as a perfect reflection of insureds' objectively measured risk profiles. For example, if health insurance premiums are set at higher levels for the wealthy than the poor for equivalent coverage, a redistribution occurs from the wealthy to the poor. Similarly, if health insurance companies are forbidden by law from charging diabetics (who have higher risks for mortality and morbidity) more for health insurance than non-diabetics, a redistribution of wealth occurs that benefits diabetics. This also means that non-diabetics will have fewer assets left to spend on other things than they would have had if the insurance were priced according to risk (and diabetics will have more). In these situations and many others like them, insurance reflects a social and political judgment about how resources *should* be distributed in society.

The redistributive impact of insurance leads to a broader observation of insurance's role as a mechanism through which the *social values and norms* of the political process are projected and manifested. As Spencer Kimball observed decades ago, "[a]ny social purpose that is felt strongly and widely enough to impress itself upon the legislature, the court, or the administrator, is a goal relevant to insurance law."[15] In this sense, insurance and the laws governing it reflect the values of the larger society in which they operate.

Most modern societies balance communitarian and individual values in a proportion determined by culture, history, and politics. The mutual-aid aspects of insurance, where individuals pool their resources together to aid the less fortunate, reflect these communitarian values. Also, the extent to which insurance is mandated for particular risks is another way these values are manifested, and prohibitions on the use of certain rating factors is yet another. On the other hand, consumers also tend to view their purchase of an insurance as an individual contract designed to protect their own interests. Thus, whenever cross-subsidies for others' losses are rejected (e.g., if a legislature or government administrator denies health insurance coverage for infertility treatments, abortions, or transgender-related health care), a kind of individualism is operating—rejecting norms of social responsibility, insisting that individuals be accountable, including financially, for their own circumstances, and sometimes condemning certain statuses or behaviors held or practiced by others.

---

15 Spencer L. Kimball, *The Goals of Insurance: Means Versus Ends*, 29 J. of Ins. 19, 22 (1962).

This mirroring of values—including the tensions among different views across an increasingly polarized political spectrum—is evident, if one searches diligently enough, in every insurance rule, principle, and issue. Returning to the example of compulsory motor vehicle liability insurance, the fact that every state in the US requires every owner of a motor vehicle to have minimum amounts of liability insurance is a statement about social responsibility for damages drivers cause others, but the low minimums required in some states show that this value is less important in those locations. In contrast, the fact that no US state requires gun owners to purchase liability insurance, and that some states prohibit insurers from adjusting homeowner policy rates based on gun ownership (but not certain breeds of dogs or trampolines owned by the household) speaks to the complex political environment and deeply rooted values pertaining to firearms in the US.[16] Health care for the indigent in the US is provided through the Medicaid program, which is essentially a government-financed health insurance system. Whenever state legislatures set the eligibility standards for this program, powerful statements are made about social responsibility and individual accountability. In short, insurance inevitably reflects the goals, values, and purposes of the larger world outside it. This important role of insurance as a tool for social regulation will receive more attention in Chapter 11.

---

16 In the US, the insurance industry, with respect to the business of insurance itself, is predominantly regulated by the states, which is different from other US industries where federal regulation is significant or predominant, and from the situation in other developed countries. This situation, which has vocal critics today, resulted from a mix of business and state regulators' pressures on Congress, which led Congress to pass a federal law in 1945 that preempted federal regulation of the business of insurance to the extent states chose to do so—as all states subsequently did. For more discussion, *see* JERRY & RICHMOND, pp. 62–85.

3 Conceptualizing insurance

As explained in Chapter 2, the predominant abstraction of insurance is contractual, i.e., insurance arises out of and is grounded in *agreements* between policyholders and insurance companies. So understood, the principles and rules of contract law, operating in conjunction with statutes and administrative rules applicable to the insurance business, provide the dominant framework for understanding the rights and duties set forth in insurance policies. But this is not the only way to conceptualize insurance, and it may be that other ways of thinking about insurance are better descriptions of what it is. This chapter explores this provocative observation.[1]

3.1 The "special kind of contract" formulation

All legal systems have rules that make defined categories of promises enforceable. In both the civil and common law traditions, one (but not the only) way to create an enforceable promise, i.e., a contract, is through an exchange of promises that creates reciprocal obligations. Insurance policies fit neatly into the contract framework (albeit with some untidiness[2]), in that the essence of the arrangement has the policyholder making

---

1 For additional discussion, see Kenneth S. Abraham, *Four Conceptions of Insurance*, 161 U. Pa. L Rev. 653 (2013) (hereafter "Abraham 2013").

2 In common law countries, some theoretical conundrums exist when, instead of two parties exchanging promises of future performances, one party trades a promise for the other's performance (instead of the other's promise) or the other's commencement of a performance (without the other making a return promise). In attempting to describe insurance contracts, some commentators have become entangled in these minutiae if the insured's side of the bargain is described as a performance (i.e., the insured makes no promise and only gives a performance in the form of paying a premium),

a promise to the insurer to pay a premium (or, alternatively, giving a performance through the present payment of a premium) in exchange for the insurance company promising to pay proceeds if, and only if, a covered loss occurs in the future.

What makes an insurance policy a special kind of contract, however, is found in certain characteristics that are quite different from a typical contract governing a sale of goods, a real estate transaction, or an employment relationship. One such distinction involves breach and remedies. In most kinds of contracts, whenever one party breaches, the aggrieved party can usually get a remedy through a cover contract (i.e., a replacement transaction that provides the same sought-after performance, with the caveat that the breacher must make up any difference between the promised performance and the cover transaction so that the aggrieved party receives the expected bargain) or an award of damages equal in value to the breacher's promised performance or the amount of the aggrieved party's loss. Given the common availability of compensatory remedies that usually make the aggrieved party whole, contract law eschews punishing contract breachers. Indeed, if a party after contracting can find a deal that is more profitable even after paying damages to the aggrieved party, contract law seemingly prefers that breach occurs. With an insurance contract, however, what the insured seeks is security, which is manifested by the insurer's promise to perform if a loss should occur, and when the insurer breaches, that promise of security is, by its very nature, destroyed. Although the insured might bring an action to enforce the insurer's performance, the mere fact that one must assert a claim to get the promised security, plus the inevitable uncertainty about whether this effort will succeed, is the very essence of insecurity. Further, the

---

or if one focuses on the fact that insurers rarely do anything (because losses are rare), which resembles the situation where an offer is extended (by the insured) and the offeree (the insurer) may or may not accept by giving the requested performance. In common law, insurance contracts are also sometimes described as aleatory, which refers to the situation where dollar values on both sides of the deal are unequal because one side's performance is heavily conditioned, as distinguished from commutative contracts where the exchange on both sides is roughly equal. None of these confusing observations is particularly useful because at its core, an insurance policy is a present exchange of the insured's promise to pay a premium, or the insured's act of making a payment of a premium, in exchange for the insurer's present and immediate promise to provide security for any future loss within coverage.

insurer knows at the time of contracting that the insured is purchasing an expectation of security, so economic efficiency can never be used to justify the insurer's nonperformance, which is not the case with most other contracts in the commercial world.

The insurance purchase is arguably distinctive in other ways that justify treating the insurance contract as a special relationship needing heightened regulation. Although insureds seek security in the face of risks that bad things will happen to them, these occurrences are unlikely to happen, and this causes insureds to lack a clear sense of what constitutes a fair price for the insurer's promise of security. Moreover, insurers use standardized forms and impose the terms therein on policyholders who have no opportunity to negotiate them and lack understanding of technical and complex policy language. Standardization, adhesive terms, and technical complexity are not unique to the insurance business; indeed, standardization helps consumers by reducing sellers' costs, thereby helping to reduce prices.[3] But the stakes of insurance contracts are so uniquely substantial that the insured needs more guidance and protection than in most other business deals consumers ever make. The content of an insurance contract and whether it is enforced may determine whether the insured can rebuild a home, provide basic support for beneficiaries after their death, continue a business, or avoid the multi-generational impacts of bankruptcy. Thus, ordinary contract principles are often distorted to the end of protecting the substantial reliance and expectations of policyholders, which is why it is sometimes said that insurance is a special kind of contract. Indeed, it might even be claimed that insurance law is a special division of contract law—or that insurance law is its own alternative category of law, separate from but closely related to contract law.

---

3 For more discussion of standardization in insurance, *see* Daniel Schwarcz, *Reevaluating Standardized Insurance Policies*, 78 U. Chi. L. Rev. 1263 (2011).

3.2 Insurance as product

The idea that insurance is more like a product than a contract is an old one. The famed contracts scholar Samuel Williston wrote in the mid-twentieth century that

> [t]he typical [insurance] applicant buys "protection" much as he buys groceries … [F]or most purposes, insurance must still be considered a contract … but it is a very special kind of contract and one currently involved in a prolonged period of popular gestation from which it may eventually emerge as a new and special form of chattel,[4] or perhaps, quasi-chattel.[5]

Today, one might analogize the purchase of insurance to the purchase of an automobile. The typical buyer of an auto (a chattel) has no concrete knowledge of how it is constructed or the technical aspects of how it works. The manufacturer assembles it pursuant to a particular design, and the buyer purchases it without understanding how the different components fit or function together. The buyer expects reliable transportation, just like a policyholder expects an insurance policy to provide protection against the risks it covers—even as the policyholder has no real understanding of how the policy is constructed, its technical aspects, its assembly or design, or the interaction of the textual components within it. One series of recent insurance advertisements in the US shows consumers visiting an "insurance store" where boxes of different kinds of insurance appear on shelves; the consumer selects a box or two and pays for them at a checkout counter,[6] directly suggesting that insurance is the equivalent of a standardized product that comes in a box, and that policyholders purchase it much like, as Williston said, they buy groceries. The fact that consumers do not bargain for the contours of a product also resembles

---

4 The etymology of "chattel" goes back centuries, but in the term's modern usage, it refers to personal property that is both tangible and movable, i.e., typically products or goods.

5 7 Samuel Williston, A Treatise on the Law of Contracts § 900, p. 34 (3rd ed. Jaeger 1963).

6 *See*, e.g., Progressive Insurance, *Someday (video)*, Mar. 16, 2015, https://www.youtube.com/watch?v=3yfFuz7Dh90. Progressive also introduced an animated insurance box in its commercials in 2012, and the box has appeared in numerous company advertisements since then. *See* Heather Taylor, *A Star is Born: Hear the Progressive Box Croon About Car Insurance*, PopIcon, Mar. 5, 2019, https://popicon.life/a-star-is-born-hear-the-progressive-box-croon-about-car-insurance/.

the adhesive nature of insurance policies, where negotiation of terms does not occur.

When the insurance transaction is understood as the purchaser buying a product or commodity, the seller (insurer) has certain obligations imposed by mandatory rules in the law of product liability. Thus, policies might come with implied warranties, such as a warranty of fitness for a particular purpose, or a warranty of merchantability, meaning that the policy is free from defects that render it unsuitable for general use. This conception helps solve the problems that emerge whenever contracts are adhesive, as is the case in insurance, but the conception would have challenges if a serious effort were made to operationalize it. Defining what constitutes a "defect" in an insurance policy would be difficult, as the fact that a policy does not cover what the insured wanted to be covered does not mean the consumer purchased a defective product. Similarly, under a contract conception, at least the meaning of a policy is determined initially by examining text in the policy; with the product conception, the policy is measured against an abstract standard of suitability or fitness, which is difficult to articulate. Insurance companies would certainly resist replacing a contract conception with a product conception, as they would claim, with considerable justification, that they do not know what the standard requires them to draft and offer to the public.

Nevertheless, just as Williston opined many decades ago, viewing insurance as a product or commodity is a meaningful way to conceptualize how insurance functions when consumers buy it to obtain security in the face of risk—just like they buy groceries, automobiles, or a smartphone.[7]

3.3 Insurance as public utility

A public utility is ordinarily defined as an organization that creates and maintains the infrastructure for an essential public service, such as water, energy supplies (gas, electricity, etc.), communication systems (phone, cable, etc.), and sometimes transportation (common carriers, operators of highways, etc.). The core idea is that the utility, even if privately owned

---

7 For more discussion, *see* Jeffrey W. Stempel, *The Insurance Policy as Thing*, 44 Tort Trial & Ins. Prac. L. J. 813 (2009).

or having features of private ownership, exists to serve the public and is expected to operate in the public interest, and thus is the appropriate subject of public supervision. Utilities are often considered natural monopolies, meaning that in the market in which they operate, services are more easily provided by a single firm because of the need for large amounts of capital investment. But this also means that the monopoly requires extensive government regulation to ensure that it operates in the public interest.

Because insurance is essential for the functioning of the economy and the reliable ordering of social relationships and interactions, conceptualizing insurance as a utility that exists to serve the public's needs and interests has plausibility. As Spencer Kimball put it, "the need for insurance became so great in twentieth-century society that insurance tended to become a kind of public utility"; he observed a "developing public attitude that insurance companies might properly be required to supply their services to all who sought them."[8] Insurance is subject to significant government regulation, which is a core characteristic of public utilities, and this factor probably more than any other drives the notion that insurance should be understood as a form of utility. Some US courts have embraced the idea that insurance has characteristics of a utility by drawing a distinction between "ordinary businesses" and the "insurance business." For example, banks, which engage in "ordinary business," are not liable for delay in acting on an application for a loan,[9] whereas a license to engage in the insurance business imposes a more robust duty to act without delay on applications for insurance.[10] If the business of insurance is "special" rather than "ordinary," the implication is that insurance is more like a utility, and thus is appropriately conceptualized as such.

Recognizing that insurance is a heavily regulated industry is important to understanding insurance law, but the conceptualization of insurance as a utility breaks down at other points. Although insurance has a robust

---

8 Spencer L. Kimball, Insurance and Public Policy, p. 7 (1960).

9 *See*, e.g., *Mfrs. Hanover Trust Co. v. Yanakas*, 7 F.3d 310, 315 (2d Cir. 1993) ("the Bank had no fiduciary duty to accept or respond promptly" on loan application).

10 *See*, e.g., *Royal Maccabees Life Ins. Co. v. Peterson*, 139 F.3d 568 (7th Cir. 1998) (applying Illinois law, "an insurance company … has an affirmative duty to respond promptly on insurance applications").

antitrust exemption in the US[11] and the EU,[12] which is characteristic of natural monopolies treated as public utilities, many aspects of insurance markets are highly competitive, which undercuts the utility conceptualization. A characteristic of public utilities is that they are required to take all comers, meaning that the utility must provide water, electricity, etc. to anyone who applies. Except for health insurance in many countries and for some product lines where the government creates a facility to guarantee insurance to high-risk applicants (such as high-risk drivers or property owners in disaster-prone areas), insurance companies are not required to accept all applicants. One might discern from this observation, however, that some kinds of insurance are more essential than others—e.g., health insurance, auto insurance upon which one's ability to engage in essential travel depends, etc.—and thus conclude that the public utility conceptualization is stronger in some parts of the insurance business than others.

3.4 Insurance as private governance

In Chapter 2's discussion of the roles of insurance, the point was made that although allocating values is understood as something governments do as part of the political process, the reality is that values are allocated via the conduct of the insurance business. For example, every time insurers decide what rating factors will be used to price insurance, some kind of social value is embedded in the choice. Some choices are, of course, more controversial than others, but, each time, a statement is being made regarding how society should be organized—which is the essence of private corporate governance. Similarly, some rating factors are plainly intended to induce human behavior, which is also the essence of governance. For example, increasing auto insurance premiums for accident-prone individuals is an effort to induce these persons to drive more carefully. Increasing premiums to owners of high-rise buildings who do not have routine inspections of structural integrity, or who do not repair identified problems promptly, seeks to encourage more responsible behaviors. Reducing premiums to homeowners who install

---

11 *See* Jerry & Richmond, pp. 62–80.

12 *See* European Commission, *Competition Policy: Insurance*, https://competition-policy.ec.europa.eu/sectors/financial-services/insurance_en.

fire alarms, who do not own bite-prone dogs as pets or have trampolines for children's play, or who install hurricane-resistant roofs and windows represents an effort to encourage specific behaviors. When applicants are denied access to insurance pools or some insureds are dismissed from the pools, the decisions stand as an expression that those behaviors which led to those decisions will not be tolerated—at least if one wants insurance coverage. Kenneth Abraham calls this, quite appropriately, a kind of "surrogate government"—that "[g]overnment in effect relies on insurers to perform some functions that government could legitimately perform but does not."[13]

3.5 Implications of the different conceptions

These alternative conceptions of insurance invite us to think of insurance in new and different ways, and this creates new possibilities for thinking about how the business of insurance should be regulated—and even what insurance law should be. The current and dominant paradigm for thinking about insurance is contract—a policy's content and performance is determined by invoking traditional and ordinary principles of contract law. But when insurance is understood as a special kind of contract, a product, a public utility, or a form of private governance, it challenges the contract law assumption that language in the agreed-upon text is binding and conclusively authoritative, and it raises the possibility that other considerations beyond language should be brought to bear to determine the scope of insurers' obligations. Further, these alternative conceptions provide a frame through which the question "how should insurance law change?" can be examined and explored.

---

13 Abraham 2013, p. 685. The use of insurance for social regulation receives more attention in Chapter 11.

4 The nature of the insurance business

4.1 The origins and rise of insurance

Long before the modern era, our ancestors understood the benefits associated with sharing risk. In many ancient societies, including those of the Chinese, Egyptians, Greeks, Romans, Hindi, Hebrews, and Christians, associations existed where members made contributions to a common fund, which was used to give assistance to the group's injured or ill, bury the dead, or assist survivors of deceased members. A commercial practice, which dates back at least to the Babylonians and the Code of Hammurabi in roughly 2250 BCE, involved the maritime practices of ancient traders who shared a vessel to travel with their goods to distant markets. Voyages in and across the Mediterranean were subject to the risk of sudden storms, and sometimes cargoes needed to be jettisoned to save the vessel. Thus, each merchant agreed at the voyage's outset (eventually, this became an implied understanding of every voyage) that if such losses occurred, each merchant at the end of the voyage, including those who suffered losses, would contribute pro rata based on the value of their goods to a fund sufficient to reimburse the losses of merchants whose cargoes were jettisoned. The mutual benefits of this risk-sharing arrangement were so obvious that it survives to the present as the principle of *general average* in admiralty law.

These mutual aid arrangements distributed risk, but they lacked the element of a transfer of risk to a third party. The Babylonians may have been the first to involve third parties when they developed what would later be known as a *contract of bottomry*. Many merchants financed their ongoing operations, including the expenses of shipping and traveling with their goods, through loans. Under the norms of that time, failure to pay a debt could result in the debtor and his family becoming indentured servants to the creditor. Thus, a disaster at sea causing a loss of all one's goods involved much more than financial devastation. A solution to prevent this outcome emerged, and it involved creditors loaning money (or goods) to the merchant at a high interest rate with the understanding that the obligation to repay the debt would be eliminated if certain events occurred that prevented the merchant from earning a profit (such as losing the goods at sea). This arrangement served two purposes. First, the creditor earned a very favorable return on the loan, and, second, the merchant had protection against the devastating consequences of a catastrophic event. The creditors paid for the losses that did occur through the high charges they levied on merchants whose voyages succeeded. The contract of bottomry also appeared in the history of the Phoenicians, Greeks, and Romans. It is possible that this contract ultimately evolved into insurance as it is commonly understood today.[1]

By the early 1100s, a small but vigorous insurance business existed in the maritime states of northern Italy, where merchant-investors assumed the risks of other merchants' losses. Merchants from Lombard (in northern Italy) introduced these practices to England sometime around the mid-1300s when they founded trading houses in London to underwrite maritime risks. Lombard Street, which still exists today in the heart of London's financial district, marks the location where many of these houses were established. Similar businesses also emerged in major financial centers that developed on the continent during the fourteenth, fifteenth, and sixteenth centuries.

By the 1600s, the practice of insuring maritime risks was common, and the acknowledged commercial center for this business was London. In the late 1600s, it was customary for shippers engaged in the maritime trade and desiring insurance to go to a popular inn in London known as Lloyd's Coffee House, and circulate among those present a slip of paper on which was written a description of the vessel or cargo, the identity of the captain

---

1 Although what happened is unknown, it is possible that medieval investors eventually realized that the risk-transfer component of the bottomry contract could be separated from the investment component; the next step would be to form risk pools based on the loss experience of larger numbers of merchants.

and crew, details of the planned voyage, and the amount of insurance desired. Those interested in insuring a portion of the risk would write beneath the description the amount for which the person was willing to be held liable in the event of loss. The term *underwriter* emerged from this practice. In 1692, Lloyd's Coffee House moved to Lombard Street, and Lloyd's of London, which is today one of the world's leading insurance and reinsurance markets, traces its history to this coffee house. However, what happened at Lloyd's and elsewhere on Lombard Street, and in other European financial centers, were private transactions among individuals, many of whom were merchants themselves.

The formation of entities resembling insurance companies occurred in the 1700s. Just as the development of maritime trade and a desire to manage the associated risks led to a demand for maritime insurance, the acquisition of property and the risk of loss due to fire led to a demand for insurance to deal with that risk. The genesis was the Great Fire of London in 1666, which destroyed roughly 80 percent of what was already one of the largest cities in the world. About fifteen years after the Great Fire, an informal organization opened at the rear of London's Royal Exchange to insure against loss by fire, and by 1690, one in ten houses in London was insured.[2] The first fire insurance company, the Sun Fire Office, was formed in London in 1710.[3]

Other products developed still later, with the common pattern being "as new risks emerge, the business of insurance will follow." The advent of railroad travel in the mid-nineteenth century—and inevitably, railway accidents—led to the invention of accident insurance.[4] Liability insurance emerged in the late nineteenth century as a corollary to the development of tort liabilities. The first liability policy was written to cover employers' liabilities to employees, but in time liability insurance was extended

---

2 *See* James Read, *How the Great Fire of London Created Insurance*, Museum of London, July 15, 2016, at https://www.museumoflondon.org.uk/discover/how-great-fire-london-created-insurance.

3 In this era, public firefighting departments did not exist, and part of the premium paid for the services of private firefighters who would respond when notified that a subscriber's home was burning. This is an early example of the role insurance companies play in loss prevention and damage mitigation.

4 *See* Adam F. Scales, *Man, God and the Serbonian Bog: The Evolution of Accidental Death Insurance*, 86 Iowa L. Rev. 173, 177–190 (2000).

to cover other types of liability.[5] Almost as soon as automobiles were invented, and especially as they quickly evolved into fast and dangerous machines, automobile insurance became available for purchase, and within a few decades automobile liability insurance became mandatory in most jurisdictions. Reinsurance companies emerged on the continent in the mid-nineteenth century, initially to provide a backstop for fire insurance companies whose portfolios consisted of highly correlated risks. The reinsurance business experienced rapid growth after World War II.[6]

Some early examples of life insurance contracts date back to the 1500s, but the product was not sold by companies until the 1700s—and then it had to overcome some popular sentiment that the product was immoral. In some countries, critics urged that it was wrong to make life the subject of a bargain (indeed, it interfered with "God's plan"), it discouraged reliance on hard work and a savings ethic, and beneficiaries would not be able to manage sudden windfalls.[7] Also, the development of financially stable life insurance companies needed to await a more fully developed understanding of the mathematics of probability and the creation of reliable mortality tables. By the 1800s, these hurdles had been overcome, and the market began to grow, with the most rapid period of expansion occurring in the twentieth century.

The origins of health insurance exist in the era of guilds in Europe. In the late 1800s, governments in western Europe (initially Germany) sought to place the operation of voluntary sickness funds under state supervision. Health insurance remains a public function in most developed countries today, although private insurance supplements the public insurance provided by state systems. In the US, health insurance is made available through a complicated hybrid system. Private insurance, which is the default, is primarily obtained as a fringe benefit in employment, but the private product is subject to significant regulation by both federal and state government. For the elderly and disabled, health insurance (i.e., hospital and medical insurance) is provided by the federal government

---

5 For more discussion, *see* Kenneth S. Abraham, The Liability Century: Insurance and Tort Law from the Progressive Era to 9/11 (2008).

6 *See* David M. Holland, *A Brief History of Reinsurance*, 65 Reinsurance News 4 (Feb. 2009).

7 *See* Viviana A.R. Zelizer, Morals and Markets: The Development of Life Insurance in the United States (2017).

(Medicare), and for the poor, it is available in most states through a state–federal partnership (Medicaid). Private health and disability insurance are predominantly post-nineteenth-century innovations.[8]

In modern times, a variety of products exist for many kinds of risks, but almost all of these are extensions from or specific applications of the major categories of coverage. This aspect of the evolution of insurance is discussed in the next subsection. The remaining subsections in this chapter discuss other aspects of the modern business of insurance.

4.2 Types of insurance

Because the universe of insurable risks is so vast and the business of insurance is so substantial, the types of insurance available in the twenty-first century defy brief summation. As explained in the prior subsection, the business of insurance evolved as new risks emerged and became important sources of uncertainty for individuals and organizations. These new risks led to the invention of new insurance products, typically sold by one company specializing in that risk, which in turn gave rise to the idea that insurance is organized and compartmentalized by *line*. For example, the line of marine insurance emerged first and became a mature line before some other kinds of insurance, like life and health insurance, even appeared. In addition, government regulation often prohibited companies from crossing into other lines. In short, the way in which the business of insurance evolved, reenforced by government regulation, led to the business becoming compartmentalized based on the kind of risk covered.

There are different ways to categorize insurance. In the most general terms, the insurance world can be divided into (a) personal insurance, which includes the types of coverages purchased by individuals and households, and (b) commercial insurance, which includes the types of insurance purchased by businesses and firms. Another approach divides

---

8 For additional discussion about the history of insurance, *see* Geoffrey Clark et al., The Appeal of Insurance (2010); Phillip Hellwege, *A Comparative History of Insurance Law in Europe*, 56 Am. J. Legal Hist. 66 (2016); Swiss Re, *A History of Insurance* (2013), https://www.swissre.com/Library/a-history-of-insurance.html; Holland, supra n. 6.

insurance into three major categories: (1) marine and inland marine; (2) life; and (3) fire and casualty. Yet another approach distinguishes between (i) first-party insurance, which covers an insured for loss of or damage to the insured's own interests, and (ii) third-party insurance, which covers an insured for liabilities arising out of the insured causing damage to the interests of third parties.[9]

Consider first the three-category categorization scheme. Marine insurance, which descends directly from the underwriting that occurred in the coffee houses and the financial centers in Europe, is a form of *all-risk coverage* (all-risk means the policy covers all forms of loss not specifically excluded) insuring ships, cargoes, terminals, and methods of transport over water and between a point of origin and final destination. Inland marine covers products, materials, and equipment transported over land (such as by truck or train).

The life insurance category includes policies that pay proceeds upon the death of the person whose life is insured, but also includes other personal policies, such as accident insurance (for accidental death or injury), health insurance (for expenses associated with medical care for illness or injury), disability insurance (for loss of income caused by illness or injury), long-term care insurance (for expenses associated with being unable to perform activities of daily living without assistance), and annuities (insurance against the risk of living too long, i.e., beyond one's economically productive years). Life insurance comes in many different varieties with distinct labels, but basically all these products fit into two categories. Term insurance is pure insurance; the coverage is for a specified duration and the beneficiaries collect proceeds if, and only if, death occurs during that term. Whole-life insurance refers to insurance that combines the term product with a savings or investment account, where some portion of the premiums are deposited and can accumulate. This *cash value* can be withdrawn, loaned, or left untouched, in which event it becomes a part of the proceeds paid upon the death of the person whose life is insured.

Fire insurance is a kind of property insurance; it covers losses caused by hostile fires (meaning fires that do not exist in a place where they are nor-

---

9 For more information and discussion, *see* JERRY & RICHMOND, pp. 33-48; Wikipedia, *Category: Types of Insurance*, https://en.wikipedia.org/wiki/Category:Types_of_insurance.

mally expected). But fire insurance companies typically write insurance in *allied lines* that cover losses due to, for example, lightning, explosion, wind, water, hail, rain, riot, vandalism, and civil commotion. Property insurance covers loss of or damage to the actual property, i.e., a physical alteration or destruction of property. It is also commonly written to cover losses tied to the loss of use of damaged or destroyed property, as happens when a residence cannot be occupied and the expense of alternative housing becomes a part of the total loss, or a factory is destroyed, resulting in a business interruption and a loss of income. This aspect of property insurance coverage is often called *time element* coverage.

Casualty insurance is primarily concerned with the insured's legal liability for injuries to other persons or damage to other persons' property. This type of coverage is typically known as liability insurance. The term casualty insurance, however, is an overworked and sometimes confusing label, because it also includes several discrete kinds of insurance, such as workers compensation insurance (coverage purchased by an employer for the benefit of employees injured, killed, or sometimes made sick on the job); fidelity and surety bonds (a kind of guarantee of obligations); burglary, robbery, and theft insurance; plate glass insurance; and boiler and machinery insurance. Accident, health, and disability insurance are sometimes categorized as casualty insurance products, but these kinds of insurance fit more logically among the personal insurance lines.

Some additional categories exist beyond those outlined above, and these perform some enormously important risk management functions. Three are particularly noteworthy. Title insurance covers defects in legal title to property, i.e., it covers the warranties a seller of property gives to the buyer that the seller possesses good title. Before the mid-1900s in the US, these warranties were usually backed, if at all, by an attorney's opinion letter that title was without defects—and the remedy for a defect ran against the lawyer who issued the mistaken opinion. The housing boom after World War II saw major growth in the use of title insurance, which was widely viewed as providing more security against the risk of defective title.[10] In recent years, title insurance has shown significant growth in Europe and many other countries around the globe, where it backs up the

---

10 *See* G. Stacy Simmons & Randy E. Dumm, *Title Insurance: An Historical Perspective*, 14:3 J. of Real Estate Lit. 293 (2006).

security provided by land registration systems and pays defense costs in the event the owner's title is later challenged.

Reinsurance is essentially insurance for insurance companies.[11] Regulators require insurers to maintain sufficient capital to pay future potential claims; however, if an insurer can transfer some of its liability for future claims to another insurer, it can reduce the amount of capital it must maintain on reserve. Also, where an insurer's pool of policyholders contains too much correlated risk, an insurer can reduce this exposure by transferring a portion of it to a reinsurer. The insurer that directly underwrites personal or commercial risk (typically called the *primary* or *direct insurer*) is said to *cede business* (i.e., transfer risk) to the *reinsurer*, which agrees to reimburse the primary insurer for its losses according to an agreed-upon formula. The primary insurer pays the reinsurer a premium for this coverage. There are two primary kinds of reinsurance: *treaty reinsurance* involves the primary insurer purchasing coverage on broad groups of policies it has issued; *facultative reinsurance* is the purchase of a policy on a specific risk that the primary insurer undertook under a single policy (such as a policy issued on a very large office building).

Microinsurance refers to low-cost insurance sold to low-income individuals generally not covered by traditional private insurance or government safety-net programs.[12] In developing countries it often works in tandem with micro-financing projects to help people in poverty obtain coverage for cattle, crops, and agricultural equipment, as well as their health and lives—essentially any risk that, if it materializes, would crush their efforts to start and maintain a business. For the poor, microinsurance is especially important because it helps avoid the collateral consequences of loss—such as spending less on food or housing, putting children to work, or selling productive assets, all of which are likely to deepen a household's poverty.

Finally, it should be noted that sometimes individuals and firms choose to carry risk themselves. This happens when a policy has a deductible or co-payment requirement, which are qualifications to a policy's limits and

---

11 *See* JERRY & RICHMOND, pp. 875–885.

12 *See* Microinsurance Network, *The Landscape of Microinsurance 2021*, https://microinsurancenetwork.org/resources/the-landscape-of-microinsurance-2021.

describe portions of any loss that the insured must bear as a perquisite to the insurer paying proceeds. At other times, individuals and firms choose not to insure at all, or not to insure first layers of potential losses and instead rely on policies that are triggered only when the magnitude of a loss exceeds the self-insured or retained initial layers. Self-insurance and retentions do not involve contracts between individuals or firms and insurance companies, but sometimes these layers are understood and functionally treated as insurance that an individual or firm provides for itself.

As noted earlier, many different kinds of specific policies exist, but these are usually extensions of one of these major categories or a combination of coverages usually found in the major categories. For example, one can purchase policies that provide travel insurance,[13] pet insurance,[14] dental insurance,[15] crop insurance,[16] event-cancellation insurance,[17] hole-in-one insurance (for a prize at a golf tournament),[18] ransom-reimbursement insurance,[19] and insurance for virtually anything else which is fortuitous and can be measured.

---

13 The coverages in travel insurance vary, but policies ordinarily provide reimbursement for vacation packages, prepaid hotel and airline reservations, etc. if a fortuitous event forces the insured to cancel the trip or the travel provider to cancel the trip without giving the policyholder either a refund or a credit for future travel.

14 This provides health insurance for a pet.

15 This provides health insurance for dental services, typically limited to teeth and gums. Other policies exist for vision, some specific illnesses (such as cancer), and prescriptions.

16 This is an important product for the agriculture industry; it can be purchased to cover crops and livestock, and can be structured as indemnity for lost product or lost revenue.

17 This product is sold to event promotors (e.g., concerts, sporting events, festivals, conferences, etc.) to cover losses if a fortuitous event forces cancellation of the event.

18 Charity golf tournaments frequently offer a large prize if a participant makes a hole-in-one on a designated par-3 hole. Tournament organizers ordinarily cover the risk that someone might win the prize through an insurance policy. This type of policy is commonly written on other similar prizes (half-court basketball shots, long-distance hockey shots, etc.), online prediction contests, and excessive and unanticipated coupon redemptions.

19 This is a policy that a firm might purchase to cover a ransom payment to secure the release of a kidnapped executive or to restore computer systems shut down by a ransomware attack.

Finally, one should note that, unless prohibited by a regulator, various types of coverages can be bundled into one policy. For example, policies for motor vehicle insurance, homeowners insurance (and renters insurance), businessowners insurance, and farmers insurance are multi-peril policies, as they combine property and liability coverages into one policy.

4.3 Insurance distribution and marketing

Historically, insurers have used intermediaries—agents or brokers—to present their products to their customers. These intermediaries are either *captive agents* (sometimes called *exclusive agents*), who sell only the products of one company, or *independent agents*, who are brokers selling the products of multiple insurers. Both are "agents" in the legal sense of principal and agent, but captive agents typically have more extensive actual authority than independent agents. Most companies also use other distribution channels, such as direct mail, telephone solicitations, on-line marketing (i.e., through websites), and e-mail. Companies that use captive agents and direct-sales methods are called *direct writers*, while companies that use brokers or independent agents are called *agency writers*.

From the insurer's perspective, the customer can be an individual person, firm, or organization, or it can be a group representative who purchases a policy for the benefit of others. The term *group insurance* refers to a plan where many individuals are covered as members of a single plan purchased by a representative of the group, usually an employer who is purchasing the insurance as a fringe benefit for employees (but the *group representative* can be a professional association, labor union, or other entity). The group representative purchases the policy (called a *master policy*) for the benefit of the members of the group, who are called *participants* or *certificate holders*. Life insurance, health insurance, long-term care insurance, disability insurance, accidental death insurance, and some other personal insurance products are frequently sold on a group basis. Group marketing is feasible for these products because they are usually sold in small amounts with limited underwriting (for example, being able to hold a full-time job is itself a good indication of good health), and with some exceptions, claims processing expenses are low (for example, a death certificate is the only evidence needed to prove death). In contrast, property and liability insurance are poor candidates for group underwriting because of the insurer's need to individually evaluate the risks before approving coverage and the necessity of doing claims processing on a case-by-case basis. In addition, in the US, the federal tax code provides employers with a tax deduction for the cost of providing health insurance, life insurance up to $50,000, disability insurance, and long-term care insurance to its employees, and also shelters employees from paying tax on the full value of the premiums paid by the employer on the employee's behalf. This encourages employers to shift some salary compensation to fringe benefits, which in turn encourages the sale of group insurance products.[20]

For centuries, the insurance business operated as a paper-driven industry; in modern times, technology and the Internet are changing how insurance is distributed (and other facets of the business as well, including claims processing and how customers shop for insurance). Websites and social media facilitate direct contact between insurers and consumers, and data show that this distribution channel is growing. But these platforms also assist the traditional broker and agent networks' search for new customers. The economies of scale associated with on-line communications is encouraging the development of specific products for affinity groups (which can be organized around virtually any subject, interest, product, service, or demographic).[21]

In the future, new technologies have the potential to completely change how insurance is underwritten, sold, and administered. Blockchain is the most prominent among these; it is a distributed and decentralized public ledger that serves as the record-keeper for virtual currencies, such as Bitcoin. This technology creates the possibility of automated smart contracting and claims processing, as well as no-contact underwriting.[22]

---

20 For more discussion of group insurance, *see* JERRY & RICHMOND, pp. 791–804.

21 For more discussion, *see* JERRY & RICHMOND, pp. 56–58.

22 *See* D. Popovic et al., *Understanding Blockchain for Insurance Use Cases*, 25 BRIT. ACTUARIAL J. e12 (2020), https://doi.org/10.1017/S135732 1720000148.

4.4 Insuring entities

The organizational structures for insurance entities vary. Most insurance is sold and underwritten by companies organized for this purpose, and these companies are of two kinds. A stock company is a corporation that markets insurance as a profit-making venture. As with any corporation, the stockholders supply the capital, pay the losses, and take the profits. In contrast, a mutual company is owned by policyholders, and the purpose is not to make money but instead to provide insurance to the members of the company. In lieu of paid-in capital to preserve solvency, the mutual company relies on accumulated surplus. Both types of companies can make a profit, but what they do with it is different; the stock company will return the profits to shareholders, but the mutual company, if the profits are not kept in reserves, can give its member-owners a refund of premium in the form of a dividend. In the US, stock companies dominate; indeed, an ongoing trend exists where mutuals are converting into stock companies. In much of the world, however, the mutual insurer is the predominant form.

Most insurance is sold and underwritten by companies, but other structures exist. The unique feature of *Lloyd's associations*, which are modeled on the original Lloyd's of London, involves individuals or capital providers (which can organize into groups usually called *syndicates*) underwriting coverage by assuming fractions of a risk offered for coverage. The underwriters pay a subscription to the association that funds the association's operations. The Lloyd's association itself is not an actual insurance company, and as such it assumes no risk nor does it function as an underwriter. Rather, the association is simply a market made up of brokers, individuals, capital providers, and syndicates, who assume risk themselves, thereby enabling those seeking insurance to find policies through the association.

Reciprocal exchanges, sometimes called *reciprocal associations*, are like mutual insurance companies but differ in the respect that firms or individuals seeking coverage join together for the purpose of exchanging risks among themselves. In other words, in the mutual company model, policyholders assume their obligations collectively in the name of the company; but in reciprocal exchanges, policyholders assume their obligations severally and cannot be held liable for more than the amount of the premium they pay for coverage.

A *captive insurance company* is typically defined as a wholly owned subsidiary created to provide insurance to its non-insurance parent company (or companies). Captives are essentially a form of self-insurance where the company is wholly owned by its insured. Virtually every kind of risk underwritten by a commercial insurer can be provided by a captive. Once established, the captive operates like any commercial insurer and must comply with state regulatory requirements applying to non-captive insurers. The captive's primary purpose is to insure its owners' risks, and the owners then benefit from the captive insurer's underwriting profits. In the US, a special kind of captive, authorized by state and federal laws, is a risk retention group, which is a liability insurance company owned by its members and which insures the risks of those members.

Standard lines insurers are, as the name implies, companies that have a license to operate and sell specific lines of insurance in a particular jurisdiction. Sometimes called *admitted carriers*, these insurers are subject to the laws and regulations of the jurisdictions in which they are licensed to operate. This type of insurer is to be distinguished from an *excess lines insurer*, also called a *surplus lines insurer*. These types of companies typically insure specialty risks for which coverage is not available from standard lines insurers. Examples include high-risk auto insureds or insureds who are not eligible for standard lines coverage due to underwriting guidelines or restrictions. In the US, standard lines insurers contribute to a guaranty fund that covers policyholders' claims when an insurer becomes insolvent or bankrupt. In the surplus lines, no requirement exists for insurers to contribute to such a fund.[23]

4.5 Alternative risk management arrangements

As discussed in more detail in Chapter 11, in recent decades, the frequency and intensity of catastrophic natural disasters have increased, challenging the ability of insurance markets to distribute risk. This has spawned efforts to identify and create alternative risk transfer and distribution mechanisms, and one such innovation involves the securitization of risk through financial instruments known as *insurance-linked securities* (ILS). ILS involve the transfer of risk from insurers or reinsurers (called

---

23 For more discussion, *see* JERRY & RICHMOND, pp. 48–55.

sponsors) to investors. The sponsor sets up a separate legal structure, known as a *special purpose vehicle* (SPV), which issues bonds to investors (typically to mutual funds but sometimes to individual investors). The proceeds from the sale of the bonds are invested in low-risk securities which serve as collateral for the bonds. Like any bond, the holder of the bond receives interest through coupon payments while the bond is in force—unless the event covered by the bond happens. In essence, these bonds constitute investors' wagers that the covered events will not happen during the terms of the bonds.

ILS cover specified risks. For example, *catastrophe bonds*, also called *cat bonds*, are the most well-known kind of ILS. First issued in the 1990s after Hurricane Andrew (in Florida) and the Northridge Earthquake (in California), cat bonds transfer the risk of losses from a natural disaster or other catastrophe from insurers to investors. If an event covered by the bond occurs, a payout to the insurer is activated, and the insurer's obligation to pay interest and repay the principal is either forgiven or deferred. This payout compensates the insurer for losses suffered from the covered event, and the investors lose their investment. If the event does not happen, the principal is repaid to the investors at the end of the bond's term, which is usually three to five years.

Cat bonds are the most common kind of ILS, but other ILS instruments are issued by life and health insurers to spread the risk of longevity, mortality, and health care costs. Cat bonds and other ILS instruments offer insurers an alternative to reinsurance and allow catastrophe and other risks to be spread to a wider set of investors. By tapping alternative sources of capital (like hedge funds, pension funds, and mutual funds), the bonds exert a downward pressure on reinsurance prices. Historically, they have provided strong returns, which has helped to attract capital into insurance markets, but they carry high risk, which is why they are not considered investment-grade bonds.[24]

Another alternative risk management arrangement involves a major change in how insurance policies are structured. For centuries, insurance has operated under a framework where the insurer reimburses

---

[24] For more discussion, *see* Steven L. Schwarcz, *Insuring the 'Uninsurable': Catastrophe Bonds, Pandemics, and Risk Securitization*, 99 WASH. U. L. REV. 853 (2022).

policyholders for damages suffered or costs incurred after an occurrence covered by the policy. Before paying proceeds, the insurer evaluates the loss in a process called *claims adjusting*, where the amount of the loss is determined so that the insurer can pay this amount, subject to policy limits and deductibles. With *parametric insurance*, which is sometimes also called *index-based insurance*, the amount of the payout is based on an objective measure of the magnitude of the covered event, instead of the amount of damage or loss suffered by the policyholder. For example, parametric flood insurance pays proceeds to the policyholder based on whether water reaches a specified number of feet above flood stage—not on how much damage the policyholder suffers. With parametric coverage for windstorm, the insurance pays proceeds based on whether wind speeds reach a certain level—not on how much damage the wind causes. The idea is that the payments do not depend on the fact of damage, but the triggering event is set at a point on the index where damages will almost certainly occur if the trigger is met.

Parametric insurance has not penetrated global markets significantly, but it is destined to receive much more attention in the future. Parametric insurance has great promise as a tool to help insure risks like natural disasters that are difficult to model. For example, the COVID-19 global pandemic demonstrated the challenges of providing coverage for business interruption losses, but one can imagine a market in which business interruption policies are issued in parametric form, and proceeds are paid whenever a trigger based on hospitalizations or deaths is reached. With parametric insurance, payouts can be faster because claims adjusting is not necessary, and policy design is more flexible because of the possibility of using different and/or multiple kinds of triggering events. Parametric insurance can also be used in reinsurance markets, where the concept is known as *industry loss warranties*. In this instance, the primary insurer seeking to transfer some of the risk purchases a contract from the reinsurer (or perhaps a hedge fund) where proceeds are paid if the total loss to the entire industry arising out of an event exceeds the designated triggering amount.

Parametric insurance is an important innovation, but it will not completely replace traditional insurance. Even when parametric coverage is purchased, a risk exists that damage or loss will occur even when the trigger is not reached, and traditional insurance will still need to exist to cover this residual risk, which is known as *basis risk*. But the availability of large data sets that enable the measuring of risk with great granularity, coupled with the efficiencies of smart contracts and blockchain technology, make parametric insurance a likely resource to cover risks that have defied effective risk management in traditional markets.[25]

[25] For more discussion, *see* Robert H. Jerry, II, *Parametric Insurance*, in COVID-19 AND INSURANCE, AIDA EUROPE RESEARCH SERIES ON INSURANCE LAW AND REGULATION (Maria L.M. Paredes & Anna Tarasiuk, eds.) (forthcoming 2023).

5 The nature of insurance law and regulation

5.1 Insurance law as a form of private law

In jurisprudence, a distinction is made between private law, which applies to relationships among individuals in a legal system (examples include commercial law, corporate law, tort law, property law, and contract law), and public law, which applies to the relationship between an individual and the government (examples include constitutional law, administrative law, and criminal law). Criminal law, for example, represents a set of public norms (e.g., murder, battery, assault, etc. are unacceptable behaviors) that are enforced by the state through state-created sanctions (e.g., fines and imprisonment). Tort law, as an example of private law, involves relationships among individuals and institutions, and sets forth rules governing those relationships and remedies for the violation of those rules. Tort law, like criminal law, involves public norms, such as the norm that individuals shall use due care and act reasonably (i.e., non-negligently) to protect the interests of others, but tort law's focus, like other branches of private law, is on the relationship between individuals.

Contract law is a type of private law, but it is unique in that the parties set the norms themselves, instead of receiving the norms from, or being subjected to imposition of the norms by, external sources. In other words, in this field of law, the parties reach an agreement about the rules that will govern their relationship, which is tantamount to the parties creating the governing law for themselves. Rules do exist in contract law that resemble rules being imposed by external sources (such as when a gap in a contract is filled with a term supplied by a statute or court, or a rule prevents proving a term that one party would like to advocate, or a contract is declared unenforceable on account of impossibility or frustration). Yet even in these instances, the rule being applied can be described as one that the law imposes because it resembles what the parties would have agreed to be their governing private law if they had taken time to think about, negotiate, and agree upon a term governing the topic.

In contract law, occasions exist where a public norm exists—such as a norm condemning overreaching, fraud, duress, unconscionability, or something else that amounts to a defect in the bargaining process—and then this norm is applied to undo an agreement or to declare that no agreement was ever formed. But the application of these norms speaks to whether the parties reached an agreement that the law should enforce, which is distinct from the "law of the agreement." When courts state that each party to an agreement owes a duty to the other to perform the agreement in good faith and to adhere to principles of fair dealing, one might say that courts are making a public norm a part of the parties' agreement, but even here, practicing good faith and fair dealing is the term that the parties would have agreed upon as their private law had they chosen to articulate a specific agreement on this point.

Because an insurance policy is a contract between policyholder and insurer, one way to understand an insurance policy is as a statement of private law created by the insurer and the policyholder. The limitation of this framing is that the insurer drafts the application on which the future insured proposes an agreement (i.e., makes the offer), and the insurer drafts the policy language which—except for policies negotiated by very large companies—is presented to the insured on a take-it-or-leave-it basis. This is the same conceptual problem that exists in any industry where standardized forms are the norm, but it is especially true in the insurance business since standardization is common in the personal lines and has very deep penetration in the commercial lines.

Understanding insurance policies as private law yields another insight. Contracts generally are not free in all respects from regulation by statute and administrative rule, and insurance policies are no exception. But because insurance policies are special in the sense that the subject of the contract is security itself, and given the pervasive and substantial reliance of individuals and firms on the promises set forth in insurance policies, it follows that the intensity of the regulation of insurance arrangements is much stronger than in other domains where contracts are used to set the rules and give order to social and economic relationships.

5.2 Regulatory entities

Available evidence indicates that all countries in the world with developed or developing economies have structures inside the governments, or acting with the authority of government, that are charged with the responsibility for regulating and supervising the business of insurance, but the structures through which this regulation is accomplished vary.[1] In some countries, the delegation is to a government agency, minister, or other official body, and in others the delegation is to an independent agency that is not a formal part of government. Some countries make a distinction between "regulation," which is understood as the making of rules and policies for the conduct of the insurance business and how companies relate to policyholders, and "supervision," which is understood as the monitoring of insurer and intermediary (i.e., agents and brokers) behaviors. Countries making the distinction typically divide the regulatory function between two agencies, whereas other countries view regulation and supervision as overlapping functions and house them in a single agency. Some countries have an independent insurance regulator (or regulators), whereas other countries place insurance regulation within a larger regulatory unit charged with financial or commercial regulation more generally. Some countries place this regulation at the federal level, whereas others devolve it to provincial or state authorities.[2] In Europe and within the EU, individual nations have their own insurance laws, with varying content. A recent project, however, has made considerable progress in stating a set of common European insurance law rules.[3]

---

1 *See* OECD Study, *Insurance Regulation and Supervision in OECD Countries, Asian Economies and CEC and NIS Countries* (1999), https://www.oecd.org/finance/insurance/1900939.pdf (reporting results of study of 29 OECD member countries, 14 CEEC and NIS countries, and 12 Asian countries).

2 For an overview of the structure of insurance regulation in 50 countries, see OECD, *The Institutional Structure of Insurance Regulation and Supervision* (2018),www.oecd.org/finance/The-Institutional-Structure-of-Insurance-Regulation-and-Supervision.pdf.

3 In 2009, a Project Group was formed to restate European insurance contract law, and within six years this group developed and published the

Interestingly, even though the US insurance industry is the largest in the world,[4] the responsibility for regulating the US industry rests predominantly with the fifty state and five territorial governments, which regulate the industry within their own borders and with their own statutes and regulations. A national association of state regulators (the National Association of Insurance Commissioners, or NAIC), which has existed since 1871, serves as a unifying influence on state regulation, including as a source of model acts and regulations, but the limitations of this decentralized structure for supervising the industry became apparent during the Great Recession of 2008 and the dramatic collapse of the largest US insurance conglomerate, the American International Group (AIG), and its ensuing USD 85 billion federal government bailout. This failure revealed sources of systemic risk that had escaped recognition by state regulators. As a result, in 2010 Congress enacted the most sweeping changes in US financial regulation since the 1930s, and one of the changes was the establishment of the Federal Insurance Office (FIO) within the Department of the Treasury. The FIO does not replace state regulation, but it has financial stability and monitoring responsibilities and represents the US in international insurance discussions.[5]

Government regulation is often understood as the activities of legislatures and administrative agencies, but this understanding of regulation is incomplete. Courts also regulate insurance through the development and

---

Principles of European Insurance Contract Law (PEICL)—Version 2015. The *Principles*, along with links to discussions of the Project, are available at https://www.ius.uzh.ch/de/research/projects/peicl/peiclinfulltext.html. For additional discussion, *see* Christian Armbruester, *PEICL—The Project of a European Insurance Contract Law*, 20 Conn. Ins. L. J. 119 (2013); European Commission, *Expert group on European insurance contract law* (undated), https://ec.europa.eu/info/business-economy-euro/doing-business-eu/contract-rules/insurance-contracts/expert-group-european-insurance-contract-law_en.

4 In 2021, the US accounted for 39.6 percent of life and nonlife direct premiums written in the world. The second- and third-ranked countries were China (10.1 percent) and Japan (5.9 percent). Europe, the Middle East, and Africa together accounted for 29.0 percent. *See* Swiss Re Institute, *Sigma*, No. 4 (2022), p. 35, https://www.swissre.com/institute/research/sigma-research/World-insurance-series.html.

5 For more discussion, *see* Jerry & Richmond, pp. 99–102; U.S. Dep't of the Treas., *Fed. Ins. Office* (undated), https://home.treasury.gov/policy-issues/financial-markets-financial-institutions-and-fiscal-service/federal-insurance-office.

application of rules in case-by-case adjudication and via interpretations and applications of statutes and administrative rules during such adjudications. When a court decides a case between two (or more) disputants, the court issues a judgment binding on those parties. However, other parties not before the court will ordinarily adjust their conduct to comply with the rules declared in the adjudicated case, as those parties are on notice of how similar cases will be decided in the future. Thus, whenever courts decide insurance cases in which they interpret contract language, apply a legal or equitable principle, determine the scope of a policy's coverage, or give reasons why an insurer's claims processing behavior is acceptable or unlawful, the court is, in fact, regulating the business of insurance.[6]

5.3 Rationales for insurance regulation

The proposition that government should regulate the insurance industry is rarely questioned; what is debated in many countries is the extent to which regulation is necessary. In countries with strong commitments to free markets and competition in the marketplace, those who advocate regulation must carry the burden of demonstrating that free markets cannot achieve stated public policy objectives. In countries with traditions of central planning (so-called "command economies"), regulation of the insurance industry is the default, and the only question is how such regulation is conducted.

Insurance regulation, like regulation in general, has the overarching purpose of serving the public's interests. Exactly what this means requires distillation, however, and multiple rationales are usually offered in support of insurance regulation. The first and arguably most important rationale is maintaining the financial stability, safety, and solvency of insurance companies. The core idea here is that insurers must have sufficient capital and reserves to meet future obligations, which in some product lines (e.g., life insurance) are long-term commitments. This means that insurers must be resilient in the face of the normal up-and-down cycles of the global economy and the unanticipated events that place additional stress on asset values and revenue flows. Part of this rationale includes ensuring

---

6 *See* JERRY & RICHMOND, pp. 114–117.

that companies do not succumb to competitive pressures that lead to inadequate rates, which if uncorrected create a risk of insolvency.

A second related rationale is ensuring policyholders are charged fair and reasonable prices for insurance. This includes preventing insurers from charging excessive rates in markets where competition is weak and engaging in discriminatory pricing by impermissibly setting rates based on factors unrelated to risk. To some extent, this rationale is inconsistent with the solvency rationale; the challenge for regulators is finding the range where stability is ensured but the product does not become unaffordable. Preventing excessive and discriminatory rates implicates a third rationale, which is preserving (and sometimes guaranteeing) the availability of coverage. This reflects the public interest in individuals and firms having access to the insurance coverages they need.

A fourth rationale for government regulation is preventing unfair practices and overreaching by insurance companies. Many examples exist in the history of the industry where market pressures (and ethical norms) were insufficient to stop insurer and intermediary practices that are highly adverse to policyholders and others who depend on the assurances of insurance policies. Thus, much insurance regulation focuses on preventing and deterring behaviors that harm policyholders and beneficiaries, such as misrepresentations and false or deceptive advertising, false statements to regulators, unlawful discrimination in sales and underwriting, unlawful inducements to purchase, settling liability claims without policyholders' consent, denying claims without reasonable investigation or processing, and many other kinds of offenses.[7]

In the EU and some other countries, promoting transparency has arguably emerged as a fifth rationale for insurance regulation.[8] The core idea here is that insurers need to provide consumers with clear, concise, and sufficient information that enables them to understand the coverage they are purchasing, compare it to other products, and make an informed buying decision. Transparency also refers to insurers' openness during claims processing and allowing access to financial information important

---

7 For more discussion, *see* Jerry & Richmond, pp. 59–62, 86–95.

8 For more discussion, *see* Pierpaolo Marano & Kyriaki Noussia, eds., Transparency in Insurance Regulation and Supervisory Law, AIDA Europe Research Series on Insurance Law and Regulation (2021).

to solvency and market stability goals. In the US, transparency is rarely articulated as a rationale for regulation. Many statutes and administrative rules do serve a pro-transparency function, but public access to information about the industry remains limited in important respects.[9] European transparency initiatives appear to be exerting an influence on US regulation; in health insurance specifically, some recent regulatory developments in the US are explicitly described as intended to promote transparency in pricing.[10]

5.4 Methods of insurance regulation

The methods through which regulation implements the above-described rationales can be sorted in different ways, but a six-category framework categorizes them well.

Financial regulation refers to those tools most directly related to the rate-making and solvency rationales, such as rate approval processes, financial reporting requirements, capital, reserve, and surplus mandates, dividend policies, investment restrictions, and rehabilitation and liquidation rules. *Licensing regulation* refers to the processes through which companies and their intermediaries (i.e., agents and brokers) are certified as being eligible to engage in the business of insurance. These processes are triggered upon commencement of insurance activities but are also required at periodic intervals when the certifications are renewed. *Product regulation* refers to the processes through which regulators enforce the content, reasonableness, and fairness of policies. *Market regulation* refers to a broad basket of tools regulators have at their disposal to ensure that insurers' sales and other trade practices, claims processing and settlement activities, and other business behaviors are fair, reasonable, and compliant with anti-discrimination standards. *Disclosure regulation* refers to a variety of tools that push information out to the consuming public and provide

---

9 *See* Robert H. Jerry, II, *Transparency in Insurance Regulation and Supervisory Law of the United States*, in Id., pp. 547–593; Daniel Schwarcz, *Transparently Opaque: Understanding the Lack of Transparency in Insurance Consumer Protection*, 61 UCLA L. Rev. 394 (2014).

10 *See* U.S. Centers for Medicare & Medicaid Services, *Transparency in Coverage* (Jan. 31, 2022), https://www.cms.gov/healthplan-price-transparency.

information to the regulators as well. These rules can serve one or more purposes in financial, product, or market regulation, and are directly relevant to transparency goals. *Consumer services* refers to what happens when insurance regulators interact with the consuming public. This includes the several ways in which regulators push out information to the public about insurable risks, insurance products, the process of purchasing insurance, what to do after a loss, claims processing practices, and other important matters. It also refers to assistance that regulators provide to consumers with complaints or concerns about insurers, brokers, agents, adjusters, and others in the insurance business.

6 Elements of an insurance contract

6.1 Overview

Insurance policies have a variety of formats, ranging from standardized agreements of modest length to highly complex negotiated agreements consisting of hundreds of pages. When negotiated, the insurer and insured are invariably sophisticated parties (typically large corporations) with expertise in insurance matters provided by the counsel of lawyers and insurance professionals. Personal insurance and the bulk of commercial insurance are provided via the use of standardized forms, which are drafted by the insurer (or an association of insurers formed for that purpose) and presented to policyholders on a take-it-or-leave-it basis, i.e., no negotiation of terms is possible. In many product lines, the policyholder can supplement the base policy with endorsements or riders that add or delete coverage found in the standard form. Policyholders can also ordinarily select from a menu of policy limits, deductibles, and sometimes coinsurance amounts, with the premium going up or down depending on whether coverage is expanded or reduced.

No universal template exists for the structure of an insurance policy, but policies tend to share several common elements. This chapter identifies and briefly discusses those elements.

6.2 Declarations page

The *declarations page* (also called a *dec page*) is the first page or one of the early pages in an insurance policy. It summarizes key information, such as the policyholder's name and address, the identity of other insureds, a description of the items or interests covered, the types of coverages provided, the policy's term (i.e., the effective and expiration dates), and the amount of coverage (including limits, coinsurance, and deductibles). The page will list the premium charged (including any applicable discounts), which will be broken down by particular coverages if the policy is priced in that manner. It will also list policy forms, riders, and endorsements, and will have the agent's or broker's contact information. The policy itself will be assigned a number for tracking purposes and may have a separate billing number, and these numbers will appear on the declaration page. It may also include policy rating and claim reporting information. In property insurance policies, if there is a lien holder, mortgage holder, or loss payee, that entity will be identified on the declarations page. Life insurance declaration pages will identify the beneficiaries and may include a schedule of benefits.

6.3 Parties and interests

At least two parties are required to form a contract; in insurance, these two parties are the insurance company and the policyholder. Sometimes a policy provides coverage to other persons or entities, such as a creditor, a member of the policyholder's household, or someone else using or borrowing the policyholder's property. Thus, there can be "insureds" under a policy who did not purchase the policy and who are not policyholders. In other words, insurance policies insure the "interests" of policyholders and insureds. (As discussed in Chapter 7, in life and property insurance, a policy is not valid if the policyholder lacks an *insurable interest* in the life or property insured.) Thus, the typical policy covers the policyholder's interests, but might also cover interests held by persons other than the policyholder.[1]

---

1 For more discussion of persons and interests protected, *see* JERRY & RICHMOND, pp. 277–340.

The declarations page will identify the person who contracted to purchase the policy and whose life, property, or other interests are covered. This person is the *named insured*. It is possible for a policy to have more than one named insured, as happens when, for example, two or more people jointly own insured property. The declarations page will also identify *additional insureds* who enjoy the coverage to the same extent as the named insured(s), although it is possible for additional insureds to be added by an endorsement to the policy. Normally this is done to reduce the additional insured's risk. To illustrate, a general contractor building a house for a landowner might add the landowner as an additional insured on its liability and builders policies, a commercial policyholder leasing retail space might add its landlord as an additional insured on the lessee's liability policy, or a general contractor retaining a subcontractor to perform a portion of a construction project might require the subcontractor to add the general to the subcontractor's liability insurance policy. Ordinarily the named insured is responsible for paying the premium, and the additional insured is not.

Examples of insureds who are not policyholders are common. In property insurance, it is common for individuals to insure property they own but which is subject to mortgage or security interests (as when an individual purchases property with funds borrowed from a lender, and the lender has an interest in the property to secure payment of the debt). The protection of the lender's interest is typically accomplished by a *loss payable clause*, which authorizes payment to a person or entity named in the policy who is someone other than the policyholder. This effectively makes the lender an insured under the policy. In property and liability insurance, it is common for the policy text to specify that the policy covers "[policyholder's name] and legal representatives." The effect of this designation is that if the policyholder should die or become incapacitated, the coverage extends to the policyholder's legal representative, i.e., the estate or legal guardian.

In liability insurance, it is common for a policy to designate the named insured and then identify other insureds through a description of classes of persons who have some relationship to the named insured. These clauses are called *omnibus clauses*, which refers to the ability of the words to refer to many categories or situations at one time. For example, an automobile liability policy might cover the designated named insured, the named insured's spouse, any family member who resides full-time in the household, and anyone using the covered auto with a reasonable belief that he has permission to do so. The core principle is that the omnibus clause creates liability coverage in favor of the omnibus insured to the same extent as the named insured.

Life insurance policies will identify both the policyholder and the person whose life is insured. The most common situation is for a policyholder to insure their own life and designate the proceeds for certain beneficiaries, but it is also common for policyholders to insure other persons' lives when they have an interest in that life (as discussed in Chapter 7; examples include spouses or partners, business partners, key employees, etc.). The person whose life is insured is called the *cestui que vie* (or CQV, meaning "he who lives"), and the CQV's death is what triggers the insurer's duty to pay proceeds.

6.4 Insuring agreement, coverage grants, exclusions, and definitions

The insuring agreement is the section in the insurance contract where the insurer states the circumstances under which it will provide coverage to the policyholder in exchange for the payment of a premium. In most policies, the insuring agreement is one or two sentences, or a short paragraph, composed out of terms defined elsewhere in the policy. Thus, the detailed meaning of the insuring agreement is obtained by reading other sections of the policy and then essentially "pouring" that content into the insuring agreement. For example, an insuring agreement might say something like this, with each of the words defined elsewhere in the policy being set off by quotations or put in bold print:

> "We" will pay for direct physical loss of or damage to "Covered Property" at the "insured location" described in the Declarations [meaning the declarations page], or elsewhere as expressly provided below, caused by or resulting from any "Covered Cause of Loss."[2]

---

2 This is an adaptation of the insuring agreement in Section I, Part A of the ISO's Businessowners Coverage Form, BP 00 03 07 13 (2012).

The insuring agreement is the core of the insurer's obligation to the policyholder. This obligation will receive further elaboration through coverage grants elsewhere in the policy, i.e., through other language that specifies what perils or risks are covered, perhaps with details about the specific interests of the policyholder that receive this protection.

Note that in the above-quoted policy language, several terms are set off by quotation marks; sometimes bold print or italics are used to draw attention to particular words or phrases. This signifies that the words within quotation marks are defined elsewhere in the policy. All policies contain a section, usually placed either at the beginning or the end, titled "Definitions." The special meanings given to these words are important because they pour content into coverage grants, exclusions, conditions, parties, interests protected, and other provisions in a policy. Any reading of a policy provision is incomplete if one of the terms has a specific definition and the "Definitions" section of the policy is not consulted.

Policies usually include other language that helps describe the coverage in terms of what is *not* covered; these provisions are called *exclusions*, and they are structured to pare back the coverage granted earlier in the policy. For example, a policy might state in the coverage grant that "damage to the insured residence caused by fire, wind, water, and hail is covered," but then say in an exclusion that "water damage caused by flood is excluded." Exclusionary language is sometimes drafted in the form of a condition, i.e., "if the water damage is caused by flood, it is not covered," in which case some commentators and courts refer to the language as a *condition*. In recent decades, insurers have tended to prefer to draft in terms of coverage rather than condition to avoid the possibility that a court will treat the language like a claims processing condition (e.g., requiring the insured to give prompt notice of loss and cooperate with an insurer's investigation), where strict satisfaction of the condition is typically not required as a prerequisite to coverage.

Insuring agreements assume one of two basic formats. The quoted version above requires that the loss be caused by a "Covered Cause of Loss." The definition of this term will link the insuring agreement to a list of specific perils that the policy covers—and only if one of those perils causes the loss will the insurer pay proceeds. This type of policy is called a *specified risk* or *specified peril policy*. If the policyholder suffers a loss and submits a claim, the policyholder has the burden to establish that one of the listed perils caused the loss. This is different from a policy where the insurer's promise is to pay proceeds if the insured property is damaged or destroyed; this type of coverage is known as *all-risk coverage*, which signifies that loss of property is covered, regardless of cause. The policyholder's initial burden with this kind of coverage is simply to establish that the policyholder owned the property and that it was damaged or destroyed. With both kinds of coverage, the insurer may have exclusions, and if the insured carries the burden of establishing coverage, then—if the insurer wishes to assert an exclusion—the burden shifts to the insurer to show that the exclusion applies. In circumstances where what caused a loss is difficult to prove, all-risk coverage is more advantageous to an insured.

6.5 Limits, deductibles, and coinsurance

An insurance policy limit is the maximum amount an insurer will pay when a loss is suffered; once the limit is reached, losses beyond the limit are the insured's responsibility. Limits are listed on the declarations page and can take different forms: a *per-occurrence limit* is the maximum amount an insurer will pay for a single event or claim; a *per-person limit* is the maximum amount an insurer will pay for one person's loss; a *combined limit* is the maximum amount that an insurer will pay for all components of a single occurrence or claim; an *aggregate limit* is the maximum total amount an insurer will pay for all occurrences or claims during the policy term; a *split limit* states different maximum limits the insurer will pay for different components of an occurrence or claim; and a *sublimit* is the maximum limit an insurer will pay for a subcategory of coverage.

In some kinds of insurance, if the covered event happens, the policy pays the limits specified in the policy without any claims adjusting process (i.e., without engaging in the process whereby the insurer investigates the loss and measures how much loss or damage was suffered). Life insurance is an example; once the fact of the insured's death is established and it is determined that no relevant exclusion applies, the insurer pays the face value of the policy. Some kinds of property insurance policies operate similarly; these are known as *valued policies*. With this type of policy, the insurer specifies the amount of coverage in the policy, and if a total loss occurs, the insurer pays those limits without any adjustment. When a partial loss happens, some valued policies will also pay a percentage of the policy limits based on the percentage that the loss bears to the total value of the property.[3]

Policy limits speak to the maximum amounts an insurer will pay, but a policy may contain limits that apply to the first dollars or first layers of a loss. A *deductible* requires the policyholder to absorb a loss out-of-pocket before the insurer's coverage begins; thus, if a policy limit is subject to a deductible of $N, any loss of $N or less is the responsibility of the policyholder. Deductibles can be written as *straight*, which means that every claim during a policy period is subject to a separate deductible, or as *aggregate*, where once the policyholder has paid out a certain amount of deductibles during a term, no more deductibles are applied to future claims during the term.

Coinsurance, like a deductible, involves loss-sharing by insurer and insured, but the difference is that the insurer and insured share all layers of the loss according to some designated percentage. For example, if coinsurance is set at 90 percent (and the coinsurance *system* is 100 percent), the policyholder bears 10 percent of all losses up to the policy limit. The amount of loss the policyholder bears will change for smaller losses if the coinsurance *system* percentage is something less than 100 percent and the insured fails to insure property for at least that percentage of its total value. To illustrate, in an 80 percent coinsurance system, the insured must cover the total value of insured property for at least 80 percent of its value to get 100 percent coverage of non-total losses, i.e., losses up to 80 percent of the value of the property. (If the policy limits are 80 percent of the total value of the property and the insured suffers a total loss, the maximum policy limit will kick in to cause the insured to bear 20 percent of the loss—even though the insured would have born no portion of losses less than or equal to 80 percent of the total value of the property.) Because most losses are small losses and total losses are relatively rarer, a rational insured will not insure the full value of property—which leads to less revenue for insurers. Coinsurance requirements seek to encourage insureds to purchase more insurance so that they avoid suffering a *coin-*

---

3 For more discussion of valued policies, *see* Peter Molk, *Playing with Fire? Testing Moral Hazard in Homeowners Insurance Valued Policies*, 2018 Utah L. Rev. 347 (2018).

surance penalty, which happens when an insured covers property for a percentage of its value less than the system's coinsurance percentage.[4]

Maximum limits serve the purpose, obviously, of constraining an insurer's liability for losses. Insurers must be certain to collect enough premium dollars and have sufficient return on capital to pay expected losses, and policy limits enable insurers to match expected losses with reserves. Deductibles and coinsurance help make this match as well, but they also have an important connection to insureds' behavior. As explained in Chapter 2, whenever insureds' potential losses are covered by insurance, a tendency exists for insureds, at the margin, to take fewer or less effective precautions to prevent loss—given that losses when covered by insurance do not affect insureds as severely as when the insureds are responsible for the losses themselves. This perverse tendency of insurance to increase losses is called *moral hazard*, and deductibles and coinsurance are important tools insurers use to respond to and manage moral hazard. To the extent the insured must share losses with an insurer or cover small losses out-of-pocket, the greater the incentive on the insured to take precautions to prevent losses. Deductibles are particularly important because most losses are small losses, not total losses, and thus, the deductible addresses the magnitude of loss insureds are most likely to experience.

6.6 Binders

Because insurers issue policies only after reviewing the prospective policyholder's application and evaluating the risk, the policy is not effective at the time of application. However, applicants typically desire coverage immediately, and insurers have an interest in extending immediate coverage to deter applicants from shopping for coverage elsewhere while the insurer evaluates the application, which is the applicant's offer and can be withdrawn at any time prior to the insurer's acceptance. Thus, it is a customary practice for insurers to authorize their agents and brokers to issue *binders* (sometimes called *conditional binding receipts*) to the applicant that obligate the insurer to pay insurance proceeds if a loss occurs before

---

4 The mathematics are not complicated, but the concept of "coinsurance systems" is difficult to grasp when first encountered. For a more detailed explanation, *see* JERRY & RICHMOND, pp. 531–536, 540–544.

the insurer acts on the application. Thus, a binder is a temporary contract of insurance that generally tracks the coverage of the proposed policy, but it exists independently of the policy and terminates when the policy is issued or the application is rejected. Usually, the binder's issuance is accompanied by the insured's payment of the first premium.

The precise coverage of the binder and its duration depends on its language. Some binders are unconditional and create full coverage from the moment the binder is issued; this is common in property and liability insurance. Some binders are conditioned on the insurer's satisfaction that the risk is insurable, which means that coverage cannot be withheld if the loss is suffered prior to the policy's issuance if the insurer, acting in good faith, would have been satisfied with the applicant's insurability. Some binders are conditioned on the insurer's approval of the application. This type of binder is the most limited; it protects the applicant from losses suffered after approval but before delivery of the policy. Conditional binders are more common in life and other kinds of personal insurance because of insurers' concern about adverse selection and the large coverage amounts frequently involved.[5]

6.7 Policyholder's obligations

Paying premiums is the core of what the policyholder does, or promises to do, for the insurer. This payment is made at or before a policy goes into effect; the premium might be paid in full or periodically in installments. For renewal, most policies have a grace period of some number of days during which an overdue payment can be made without an interruption of coverage; sometimes this provision is mandated by statute or regulation. If a loss happens during the grace period, the typical practice is that the insurer deducts the premium from the proceeds paid to the insured. If the policy lapses (i.e., if the grace period expires without a payment of premium), the coverage lapses, but a reinstatement process may be available. This process resembles the application process, although the insurer's evaluation of the risk and the policyholder will likely be less rigorous. The insurer also has the option to refuse reinstatement, which differs from the

5 For more discussion, see JERRY & RICHMOND, pp. 185–193.

grace period apparatus, where coverage is continuous if the premium is paid during the grace period.

The architecture of the policyholder–insurer agreement is essentially this: "We [the insurer] will provide the insurance described in this policy in return for the premium and the policyholder's compliance with all applicable provisions of this policy." The means that if the policyholder does not pay the premium or fulfill other policy obligations, the insurer is not obligated to perform if a loss within coverage occurs. Yet payment of the premium is not a contractual duty in the same sense as in an ordinary contract, where, for example, a party who contracts to buy beans is obligated to perform on the agreed date for performance by tendering payment—and is vulnerable to a claim for damages if this duty is not performed. This is because the insurer cannot sue and recover damages for the policyholder's nonperformance of the duty (or otherwise enforce it). Instead, in insurance, the policyholder's duties are something the policyholder must do as a condition to the insurer being obligated to perform, i.e., to pay for the insured's losses within coverage. An aggrieved contracting party's suspension of performance is a standard response to a material breach (and nonpayment of premium easily meets the materiality test); for the insurer when the policyholder does not perform, this is the only response, and the only one insurers need.

Insurance policies impose other duties on insureds. For example, the insured has certain procedural duties after the insured event occurs, such as giving reasonably prompt notice of the event to the insurer and documenting the circumstances surrounding the loss. One of the most important policyholder duties is cooperating with the insurer. This includes responding fairly and honestly to all the insurer's reasonable requests about a claim and providing throughout the term of the policy information or reports that the policy requires. Property insurance policies require an insured to take reasonable steps to mitigate a loss after it occurs (although they also typically provide that the costs of that mitigation are included in the loss that the insurer will indemnify).

In insurance, courts and commentators do not have a consistent vocabulary for whether certain policyholder obligations are described as "duties" or "conditions." Some of this happens because it is common for insurance policies to list policyholder duties (such as the duty to cooperate, the duty to give notice of loss within a reasonable time, and the duty to file a proof of loss) in sections of the policy titled "Conditions." This is not inconsequential, because the contract law rule is that express conditions must be strictly satisfied, subject to some exceptions that are sometimes used to prevent a contracting party's forfeiture. With the duty to give prompt notice of loss, for example, the possibility of forfeiture is front and center, because if a notice of loss requirement is imposed strictly when an insured is only a few days late with a notice, the insured is vulnerable to losing coverage and suffering the full impact of a loss, which is the essence of forfeiture. This is the reason courts frequently hold that an insurer cannot deny coverage for late notice unless it can demonstrate it suffered material or substantial prejudice from the delay. Interestingly, this outcome is consistent with general contract law; if the prompt notice requirement is viewed as the insured's duty (and not a condition to the insurer's duty to perform), then the insurer is entitled to suspend performance only if the insured commits a material breach, which cannot be said to have happened when the insurer does not suffer prejudice.

Not every provision in the section called "Conditions" involves a policyholder duty, however. Many simply explain various aspects of the parties' relationship to each other and how the policy works. These provisions will vary depending on the type of coverage involved, but some may be, for example, explanations of how the extent of insurable interest limits the insurer's duty to pay, how proceeds paid to an insured are calculated and settled, the impact of the insured having coverage from other insurers applicable to the same event, the process for resolving any disputes between insured and insurer, rules governing shared interests in covered property, rules governing multiple insureds being liable for the same loss, the impact of an insured's concealment or fraud, rules on cancellation and nonrenewal, the insurer's subrogation rights, whether the policy is assignable and, if it is, how that is done, and other terms depending on the type of coverage.

6.8 Insurer's obligations

From the insured's perspective, the insurer's duty to pay proceeds in the event of loss is the most important duty an insurer undertakes. In first-party insurance (property and the personal lines), obtaining security from risk of financial loss is the reason the policyholder purchased coverage in the first place. The duty to pay proceeds is often called the *duty to indemnify*, given that the payment of proceeds protects against damage or loss. In liability insurance, the insurer promises to indemnify the insured for sums the insured becomes legally obligated to pay to third parties. The liability insurer usually pays these sums directly to the third parties to whom the insured has become legally obligated, but in so doing, the insurer protects the insured from a reduction in assets that would occur if the insured made this payment. Thus, the duty to pay proceeds in liability insurance also functions as indemnification for the insured's loss, even though the payment is made to a third party to compensate for that party's loss.

In both personal and commercial liability insurance, the insurer undertakes a second important duty in addition to the duty to indemnify. The liability insurer also assumes a duty to defend the insured in any lawsuit brought by a third party against the insured in which the plaintiff alleges a liability within the policy's coverage. The duty to defend is very valuable to insureds; in many situations where an insured is sued, the most significant expense is not indemnity—and this is most obviously true when the insured has, in fact, no liability to the third party—but is instead the cost of preparing and executing a defense to the claims made against the insured. When the insurer takes responsibility for appointing and paying counsel to defend the insured, the insurer provides the insured with an extremely valuable form of security.

Both the duty to indemnify and the duty to defend are contractual, as they are explicitly mentioned in insuring agreements. In first-party insurance, the indemnity promise will be stated in words such as "we [the insurer] will pay for any loss ...." In liability insurance, the indemnity promise will be stated in words such as "we will pay those sums the insured becomes legally obligated to pay as damages because of [covered perils] to which this insurance applies ...." The defense promise in liability insurance will be stated in words that reference back to the duty to indemnify, such as "we will have the right and duty to defend the insured against any suit seeking those damages."

Contract law has long recognized that a reciprocal duty of good faith and fair dealing is implied in every contract, but this principle has had enormous influence in insurance law. Courts explain and apply this duty of good faith in various ways, but it is commonly said that the insurer owes a duty to the insured to conduct itself with the *utmost good faith* for the benefit of its insured, with failure to do so amounting to the insurer's *bad faith*. Many courts have gone beyond contract law to anchor the duty in tort law, which creates the possibility of holding an insurer liable in tort for bad faith performance of their contract obligations. Initially, many of these cases involved insurers' claims settlement practices in liability insurance, but some courts extended the rule of these cases to first-party insurance settings where insureds successfully argued that insurers had acted recklessly or egregiously in denying or mishandling their claims. Because tort law allows a broader range of consequential damages than contract law, has a less restrictive foreseeability-of-the-damages requirement, and has much greater potential for the award of punitive damages, these extensions are significant. From a policyholder perspective, these extensions are needed to deter insurer misconduct in a setting where the contracts serve vital public interests and the usual contract remedies are insufficient to deter such misconduct. From an insurer perspective, these extensions generate unjustifiably large judgments that make insurance more expensive and less available.

Describing exactly what constitutes a lack of good faith has proved elusive, and no generally accepted definition exists. What does seem clear is that an insurer simply being mistaken is not enough to show bad faith, nor is the mere fact that the insurer breached the contract a conclusive demonstration of bad faith. Rather, the insured must demonstrate something in the order of the insurer lacking any objectively reasonable basis to support its decision or action. When malicious, dishonest, reckless, intentional, or oppressive behavior is proved, a finding that an insurer breached the duty of good faith is most likely.[6]

---

6 For more discussion, *see* JERRY & RICHMOND, pp. 147–160.

7 Fundamental assumptions of insurance (and their limits)

7.1 Fortuity

Because the essence of insurance is a policyholder paying an insurer to assume the policyholder's risk of an uncertain future loss, it follows from this uncertainty premise that the loss must be accidental in some sense to be insurable. This requirement is the essence of the fortuity principle. In its most common applications, the principle means that losses that have already occurred, are in the process of occurring, or are certain to occur are not losses an insurer can assume under a valid contract of insurance. This principle, however, frays at its edges.

Whether a loss is fortuitous depends on whose viewpoint is used to describe it. In property insurance, fortuity is almost always evaluated from the viewpoint of the person whose interest is insured. Thus, if the insured intentionally destroys insured property, the loss is not fortuitous. (Note also that policy exclusions invariably take this kind of loss outside the coverage, but the fortuity principle provides an independent basis for an insurer denying coverage.) The insured who intentionally chooses not to take reasonable steps to mitigate loss as a loss unfolds does not suffer a fortuitous loss. Under the fortuity principle, a person cannot suffer a loss and then subsequently purchase insurance to cover it. Similarly, when a loss is underway, a person cannot purchase insurance covering it—but if the applicant is unaware that the loss is occurring at the time insurance is secured, the loss is fortuitous.

In life insurance, the analysis unfolds slightly differently. A policyholder who insures his own life and then commits an act of intentional self-destruction (i.e., suicide) does not suffer fortuitous loss from his viewpoint, but such an occurrence is fortuitous from the beneficiaries' viewpoint—assuming the beneficiary played no role in causing the insured's death. Insurers have a valid concern about individuals purchasing insurance while concealing a plan to take their own lives to enrich their beneficiaries or preserve a threatened family asset, and thus it is routine for life insurance policies to exclude coverage for suicide for a period, usually one to three years, after the policy's issuance. However, the fortuity principle is applied in life insurance suicide cases in a way that supports the validity of life insurance contracts, thereby serving the important public interests furthered by such policies.

In liability insurance, the insured's intentionally caused harm to a third party is not fortuitous from the insured's viewpoint, although it often is from the victim's perspective. Although there is some limited authority for using the victim's perspective in some circumstances, the substantial weight of authority uses the insured's viewpoint to determine fortuity. Virtually all liability policies have intentional act exclusions that lead to this result anyway, but a few rare situations exist where the intentional act exclusion does not take a voluntary act outside the coverage, and in these situations the fortuity principle may have independent force and lead to a no-coverage result.

The apparent simplicity of the fortuity principle—a loss must be accidental in some sense to be insurable—hides some subtle difficulties. Consider life insurance, for instance: since death is certain to occur in the future, how can it be insurable consistently with fortuity? The answer is that although death is certain, its timing is uncertain, which is enough to supply the element of fortuity to satisfy the principle. With property, depreciation and ordinary wear-and-tear are certain to occur, and thus it would seem that replacement cost coverage violates the principle of fortuity. Although this question initially vexed those grappling with whether to allow replacement cost coverage when it was first suggested, regulatory authorities and courts upheld the replacement-cost product under the reasoning that depreciating an expensive asset (like a home) is likely to leave an insured unable to rebuild or replace if depreciation is not covered, and the uncertainty of this kind of hardship is enough of a link to fortuity to provide a basis for recognizing the validity of this economically important and highly desirable coverage.

The significance of the fortuity principle in operation is found in what are called the *nonfortuity defenses*. Essentially three kinds of nonfortuity defense exist, although there is some overlap in these categories. The *known loss defense* refers to situations where the insured knows or should know that a loss has already occurred at the time the policy was issued. Naturally, factual disputes commonly arise over whether the insured knew, or should have known, that a loss had already occurred or had a substantial probability of having already occurred.

The *loss in progress defense* refers to situations where a loss is in the process of occurring at the time the insured purchases coverage. If persons were able to purchase insurance when loss is imminent or already underway, they would wait to purchase their first insurance until a loss was about to occur, which would prevent risk pools from being formed and functioning effectively. (Insurers also address this circumstance on their own by suspending the sale of insurance when losses are looming, as happens with homeowners insurance when a hurricane has formed over the ocean and is headed toward land.)

The *known risk defense* is the most problematic of the nonfortuity defenses. Taken literally, this defense would invalidate insurance, in that the reasons people purchase insurance is because they are aware of the risks they want to insure. When this label is used, it should be understood as referring to a category of risks that the insured knows are substantially likely or probable to produce a loss, thereby making it appropriate to treat knowledge of these risks in the same category as one would treat knowledge of a loss that has already occurred.

Much of the work of the fortuity principle is done by intentional act exclusions, which are discussed in Chapter 9. However, this principle is distinct from the policy exclusion, and thus is applied independently to determine whether a policy can validly cover a particular risk.[1]

---

1 For more discussion, *see* JERRY & RICHMOND, pp. 368–376.

7.2 Insurable interest

7.2.1 The rationale

The origins of the insurable interest doctrine are found in a customary practice in eighteenth-century English marine insurance, where someone seeking insurance was not required to demonstrate ownership of or some other legal relationship to the ship or cargo for which insurance was sought. When someone has an economic or personal interest in a piece of property, it is likely that this person would not want that property to be destroyed or damaged. But if a person can insure something in which they have no interest, such as someone else's property, the incentive to destroy that property to collect the insurance is apparent. The same analysis holds for a life in which one has no interest, such as the life of a stranger. The insurable interest requirement seeks to prevent the destruction of property and lives that is incentivized for unscrupulous insurance purchasers in the absence of such a requirement.

The insurable interest requirement first appeared in a 1746 Act of Parliament (GBR) that addressed the practice of insuring ships and cargoes without an ownership interest or some other legal relationship to the property. The preamble to the Act stated that the lack of any such requirement had caused "many pernicious practices, whereby great numbers of ship with their cargoes, hath either been fraudulently lost or destroyed, or taken by the enemy in time of war …."[2] The Act declared "null and void to all intents and purposes" any policy written without "proof of interest" or "by way of gaming or wagering." Later in that century, similar gaming practices developed with respect to insuring lives, and a 1774 Act declared void any policy of life insurance issued in circumstances where the "person or persons for whose use, benefit, or on whose account such policy or policies shall be made, shall have no interest, or by way of gaming or wagering."[3]

The insurable interest doctrine has carried forward into modern insurance law, and two purposes are attributed to it. The first is discouraging the use of insurance as a mechanism for gambling or wagering. In most countries, gambling is not considered immoral, irreligious, or a vice;

---

2 Act of 1746, St. 19 Geo. 2, c. 37 § 1 (Eng.).
3 The Life Assurance Act of 1774, 14 Geo. 3, c. 48 (Eng.).

indeed, many governments sponsor state-administered lotteries. Thus, prohibiting the use of insurance as a subterfuge for gambling or wagering must rest on other logic, and economic productivity provides the analysis. When two (or more) people make a bet or wager, nothing is created; the bet simply transfers wealth among the betting parties without creating anything new (although bets and wagers do create value for those who facilitate them and have earnings because of them, e.g., governments running lotteries and the owners of casinos—but this value is simply a slice of a valueless transaction). Insurance creates value by enabling the transfer of risk; the amount of the premium exceeding expected loss is the value of the security derived by the policyholder. The insurable interest doctrine represents a public policy that insurance contracts should not be used as a subterfuge for economically valueless transactions. Yet if economically valueless transactions do no harm in and of themselves, the question of why they should be prohibited remains. The explanation is found in the second and arguably more important purpose. Requiring an insurable interest removes the incentive for the procurer of the insurance to destroy the subject of the insurance, i.e., someone's property or life. This is one dimension of moral hazard, which is the tendency of insurance to increase loss (and which was discussed in Chapter 2).

In practice, few reasons exist to think that insurers deliberately issue policies in which insurable interests are lacking, as this disrupts the calculations upon which insurers' risk pooling decisions are based. Thus, when the doctrine comes into play, it is typically because either the insurer was unaware that the insured lacked an insurable interest, or other reasons exist for invalidating coverage and the insurer is having difficulty proving them, causing the insurer to resort to the insurable interest defense in an effort to deny coverage. In life insurance, the doctrine sometimes surfaces when the insured's beneficiaries or heirs dispute who is entitled to proceeds of a policy.

7.2.2 Operationalizing the doctrine

The principle that an insurable interest is required for an insurance policy to be enforceable depends on the meaning of "interest." "Interest" is sometimes defined by statute; absent a statutory definition, courts define the term.

In property insurance, two alternative tests are used—the *legal interest test* and the *factual expectancy test*, with the latter having a growing number of adherents. A legal interest is ordinarily understood as including any kind of property right that the law recognizes, ranging from ownership rights to equitable rights to possessory rights. Also, a contract right which depends upon the existence of property (such as when a lender takes a security interest in property to secure a loan made to a borrower) is a legal interest that enables someone who does not own the subject property to insure it. Although this situation is rarer, if a person would suffer a legal liability in the event non-owned, non-possessed property is lost or damaged, that person has an insurable interest in the property.

A factual expectancy is the expectation of economic advantage if the insured property continues to exist, or, conversely, the expectation of economic detriment or loss if the insured property is damaged or destroyed. The factual expectancy test is broader than the legal interest test because it does not depend on the presence of a technical legal connection to the property. Also, the factual expectancy test is more closely connected to the insurable interest doctrine's purpose—because it is the insured's factual expectations, not the presence of a technical legal interest, which deter wagering and the destruction of property. Under the logic of this test, the presence of the insurable interest is measured at the time of loss because a person having an insurable interest at that time is not likely to destroy the property for a windfall gain, which might not be the case if the insured were only required to have an insurable interest at the time of contracting.

In life insurance, the explanation of "interest" begins with the observation that everyone has an unlimited insurable interest in their own life. As a practical matter, insurers will not sell an unlimited amount of insurance to an individual because at some point moral hazard concerns—i.e., intentional self-destruction—become too severe, revealing that insurers treat lives as having finite economic value that sets a limit on the amount of coverage they will sell. As for insuring the lives of others, in familial relationships the test typically turns on the degree of the relationship. In the immediate family, spouses and partners have an insurable interest in the lives of each other, and parents have insurable interests in the lives of their children. Beyond these degrees of relationship, the authorities are inconsistent on whether an insurable interest exists. The rule is sometimes described as a *love and affection test*—i.e., whether the relationship is close enough that love and affection are sufficient to supply the insurable interest.

Apart from the degree of relationship test, the presence of an economic interest in the life of another will support an insurable interest. Thus, if a person is likely to suffer an economic loss because someone's death would cause financial loss, that person has an insurable interest in the insured life. Under this logic, a business has an insurable interest in the life of a key employee, business partners have insurable interests in the lives of each other, and a creditor has an insurable interest in the life of the debtor (but, under the better reasoning, only up to the amount of the debt).

In life insurance, it is commonly said that the insurable interest must exist at the time of contracting. Although this rule departs from the property insurance rule, the reality in life insurance is that the incentive to murder appears in situations where someone takes out insurance on the life of another and designates oneself as the beneficiary. Requiring an insurable interest at the time of contracting addresses that possibility directly.

7.2.3 Recurring issues at the boundaries

Like the fortuity principle, the insurable interest doctrine frays somewhat at its edges. Consider, for example, property insurance purchased by good faith purchasers of stolen goods. The good faith purchaser has no legal or equitable title to the property, and only has a right of possession that will be extinguished if the true owner appears and reclaims it. Under strict application of the legal interest test, the good faith purchaser would seem not to have an insurable interest, unless a possessory right subject to easy extinguishment qualifies. However, the good faith purchaser, who by definition had no reason to know the property was stolen at the time of purchase, has a lawfully acquired ownership interest which is good against everyone in the world except the true owner. The factual expectancy test handles this issue more easily, because the good faith purchaser would clearly suffer an economic detriment if the true owner reclaimed the property, and no public norm is violated if the good faith purchaser is allowed to insure this interest.

In life insurance, a question that has proved perplexing is whether a policyholder who insures their own life can assign the policy to a new owner who does not have an insurable interest in the policyholder's life. From one perspective, because a policyholder can designate as a beneficiary someone who lacks an insurable interest in the policyholder's life, it should be permissible to assign a policy to someone lacking an insurable interest. In both situations, the policyholder consents to someone lacking an interest having a claim on the proceeds, and a knowing assignment seems to have no greater moral hazard concerns than the beneficiary designation. In addition, free assignability of insurance policies arguably maximizes the value of policies as an asset. On the other hand, a policyholder purchasing a policy and then assigning it to a stranger is functionally the same as a stranger lacking an interest purchasing the policy in the first instance, which is not what the insurable interest doctrine allows. Indeed, if the assignment was part of a plan formed pre-purchase to circumvent the insurable interest rule, i.e., if the assignment was part of the assignee's plan to make a wager, voiding the transaction seems appropriate. Thus, when a purchase of a policy is followed immediately by an assignment, an inquiry into the bona fides of the transaction is appropriate if someone with an interest in the proceeds requests it.

In the foregoing situations and others like them where the insurable interest doctrine is implicated, the overarching question is whether the insurance arrangement is a bona fide transaction for risk transfer and distribution, or whether it is an effort to disguise a wager as insurance, thereby circumventing the insurable interest doctrine and raising the moral hazard concerns the doctrine is designed to mitigate.[4]

7.3 Indemnity

7.3.1 The principle

The core of an insurance contract is security, which refers to the insurer's promise to reimburse the insured for its loss—i.e., indemnifying the insured against the consequences of loss. Thus, the indemnity principle plays an enormous role in insurance. In property insurance, the indemnity principle controls the calculation of proceeds to be paid to the

---

4 For more discussion of the insurable interest doctrine, *see* JERRY & RICHMOND, pp. 233–276.

insured. In life insurance, the indemnity principle is weak, but in other lines of personal insurance, such as disability and health insurance, the principle is strong. Indemnity requires reimbursing the insured for losses suffered, but nothing more. The indemnity principle is not violated if the insured receives less than the full amount of loss, but it is violated if the insured profits from the loss-producing event.

The language in property insurance policies typically carries forward the indemnity principle by articulating the insurer's obligation to pay for loss as a set of alternative measurements, with whatever produces the smallest amount being the measure that is used. The alternatives are usually cast as: (1) the policy limits stated on the declarations page; (2) the amount of the insured's interest in the property at the time of loss; (3) the value of the property at the time of loss; and (4) the cost to repair or replace the property with property of like kind and quality. The policy limits, of course, always serve as a cap on recovery, and the other three limitations work together to ensure the policyholder does not profit from the occurrence. The second limit, the interest limit, can be understood as a particularized application of the insurable interest doctrine; the amount of the insurable interest places an upper limit on what the insured may recover. The third limit, the value limit, essentially states that the insured should not—and ostensibly will not—end up better off after the payment of insurance. The fourth limit, the repair or replace limit, backs up the third limit by stating that in a case of partial loss, the insured is only entitled to have the damage repaired, and if the loss is total, the insured is only entitled to a replacement with property of like kind and quality. When an insurer pays the insured proceeds for a property's total loss, the insured receives the equivalent of the property's full value. This means, then, that the insurer, having paid for the property in full, becomes the owner of what is left of the property, which will be the property's salvage value. Salvage value can at times be significant, so it may be that the insured will desire to buy back that value by accepting less than a payment for total loss.

Under the fourth limit, the insurer has the option to replace property (with like kind and quality) when the property is a total loss. This addresses the moral hazard concern that an insured who needs cash may attempt to arrange for the property's destruction, escape detection (because intentionally destroying one's own property is not a fortuitous loss and is also excluded from coverage), and then collect proceeds, i.e., essentially convert an illiquid asset to cash. When loss is partial, the concern is the same, as an insured might opt to keep the cash and not make the repair, thereby securing some liquidity at the insurer's expense. Insurers address this possibility in the partial loss situation in several ways. For repairs, it is common for the insurer to issue a reimbursement check jointly to the insured and to a repair business, which means the check will not be cashed unless the repair is done. Another alternative is for the insurer to pay a percentage of the cost of repair and then pay the remainder when the repair is completed. Another approach, which is often used when damage is caused by something outside the control of the insured (such as weather), is to pay proceeds to the insured equal to the amount of the damage, but to make no payments for subsequent damage unless the insured can prove that the proceeds were used to repair the original damage.

The "like kind and quality" limitation also seeks to affirm the indemnity principle, in that the language states that the insured cannot receive a repair that improves the value of the damaged property. Some policies also contain a *betterment clause*, which states that if a repair or replacement results in better than "like kind or quality," the insurer will not pay for the net improvement. The "like kind and quality" limitation has been controversial in automobile insurance. When a vehicle has been in service for a few years, its value is depreciated, and "like kind and quality," from the insurer's perspective, means that damaged parts can be replaced with depreciated or used parts, or with new but non-"original equipment manufacturer" (OEM) parts. Insureds, however, have argued that non-OEM parts are substandard and that the "like kind or quality" promise can only be fulfilled with the use of OEM parts. After insureds prevailed in some, but not all, of these disputes, insurers have modified policy language to make clearer the insurers' responsibilities regarding the kind of parts that may be used when making repairs.

In life insurance, the principle of indemnity is weak because, obviously, lives are different from property and lack a market value, notwithstanding that economists have techniques for putting statistical values on lives. Although the legal rule is that the amount of insurance an applicant can obtain on their own life is unlimited (given that one has an infinite insurable interest in one's own life), as a practical matter, insurers place limits on the amount of insurance they will sell to individuals, which means that insurers do engage in at least a rough valuation of lives. To illustrate, if a person with little income or wealth, few assets, and moderate to significant debt sought to purchase $15 million of insurance on her life, the insurer would balk under the logic that this applicant does not need that much coverage. Moreover, the insurer would suspect that this applicant has knowledge about facts and circumstances not known to the insurer (i.e., information is asymmetrical between applicant and insurer). Perhaps the applicant has knowledge that she has a serious illness that will soon end her life and this information is not known to, or is not being shared with, the insurer. Perhaps the applicant is contemplating intentional self-destruction in a few years and has a plan to use the proceeds to clear debt and provide a substantial gift to beneficiaries. When the insurer declines to issue insurance to an applicant because the amounts sought are excessive, it is as if the principle of indemnity is operating in life insurance, even if the principle is formally inapplicable.

When a life insurance policy is issued, the policy will stipulate the amount of proceeds to be paid in the event of the insured's death. Some policies have provisions that pay double the face value in the event the insured dies in an accident; somewhat curiously, these policies are often called *double indemnity policies* even though the principle of indemnity is weak in life insurance.

Despite the strength of the indemnity principle in property insurance, it is not controlling in all property policies, in that some kinds of property insurance policies pay stipulated values in the event of loss. For example, *valued policies* are common in marine insurance; they stipulate the value of a vessel or cargo and provide that the insurer will pay this amount if the property is totally destroyed. A similar product exists in some states in the US where statutes bind an insurer to pay the policy limits when a structure suffers a total loss due to certain kinds of perils. The ostensible purpose of these statutes is to prevent insurers from selling large sums of coverage but then claiming after a loss that the structure was not worth as much as the policy limits and then capping the amount of proceeds paid to this reduced value. The critique of these statutes is that they encourage insureds to seek and obtain coverage exceeding a structure's value, which creates an incentive to destroy the property, try to avoid detection, and then collect the inflated amount. Valued policy statutes make it incumbent on the insurer to investigate the property carefully during underwriting and make sure that the insured amount accurately reflects the property's value. In short, valued policy statutes essentially suspend the indemnity principle.

When *replacement cost coverage* was created in the 1960s, it was necessary to reconcile this type of coverage with the indemnity principle as it was then understood. Property has a useful life; usually, value declines during that period until the end of it, when the property has no remaining value. If property can only be insured for its *actual cash value*, which is usually defined as replacement cost less depreciation, the insured always suffers an out-of-pocket loss if fixing the damaged property requires replacing it with new property. From one perspective, measuring the insured's loss by replacement cost produces a betterment when depreciated property is lost or damaged, which violates the principle of indemnity. Indeed, if the insured were a business, received replacement cost as the recovery, and then chose to go out of business, the betterment is obvious. But from another perspective, if the business wished to continue operating as a going concern, the only way to indemnify the insured is to replace the property it needs to continue to operate, and thus in this context replacement cost coverage is arguably the truest form of indemnity. Because replacement cost coverage serves an important and valuable purpose, especially for homeowners who frequently lack the resources needed to repair or rebuild after major damage, those who advocated for the product eventually succeeded in overcoming the arguments advocated by those adhering to a strict understanding of indemnity.[5]

7.3.2 Subrogation

Subrogation is a right that enables one who is secondarily liable for a debt and then pays it to succeed to the rights that creditors hold against the debtor. The source of the right can be a contract (such as an insurance contract), a statute, or the law of equity. This means that subrogation can exist as an equitable remedy even though no contract or statute allows it, but it is also possible that a contract or statute can supersede, i.e., preempt or modify, rights bestowed by equity, including subrogation. Subrogation is important in insurance because it enables the insurer to "stand in the shoes" of the insured and assert the insured's rights against a responsible third party. To illustrate, suppose a third party damages the insured's property and is legally responsible for the damage under tort or statutory law. The insurer pays for the insured's losses under the insurance policy, which binds the insurer contractually. Having involuntarily

5 For more discussion of the indemnity principle, *see* JERRY & RICHMOND, pp. 536–554.

paid the wrongdoer's debt to the insured under the legal compulsion of the contract (and being secondarily liable for that debt), the insurer (the subrogee) is subrogated to the rights of the insured (the subrogor) against the third-party debtor (the wrongdoer, with respect to whom the insured is the creditor). If the subrogation right is successfully asserted, the insured will be fully reimbursed (through the insurance contract), the insurer will be made whole (the sums it paid to the insured will be reimbursed through the recovery from the wrongdoer), and the loss will fall on the party who is responsible for it (the wrongdoer). Note that if the wrongdoer has a valid policy of liability insurance, the loss will fall on the wrongdoer's insurer.

Successful assertion of a subrogation right in the foregoing examples causes two things to happen. First, subrogation enables the loss to fall on the person who is legally responsible for causing it, instead of the party who pays the debt (i.e., the insurer). This is important as a matter of justice because parties who are legally responsible for debts are the ones who should pay them. The mere fact that someone else pays the debt should not absolve the debtor from responsibility. Note, however, that it is not in the public interest for a plethora of volunteer debt-payors to search for unpaid debts owed by others, pay them, and then pursue the debtors in the style of self-appointed bounty hunters. Thus, for subrogation to be available, the subrogee must assert the right under some kind of legal compulsion, which ordinarily is a contractual obligation to perform as a surety or insurer. Second, subrogation prevents the party to whom the debt is owed (the insured) from receiving a windfall—and thereby promotes the principle of indemnity. In the foregoing example, if the insured were allowed to recover from both the insurer and the wrongdoer, the insured would receive a double recovery. But if the insurer as subrogee succeeds to the insured's rights against the wrongdoer, the insured recovers only once (i.e., is made whole), and the insurer is reimbursed for the payment it made to the insured. Moreover, making the insurer whole benefits other insureds in the risk pool in which the injured insured participated, because when proceeds paid out of the pool are reimbursed, premiums can be kept lower, at least in theory, for all participants in the pool.

Subrogation is common in property insurance, given that in property insurance the indemnity principle is strong and the idea that insureds should not profit from their losses springs from this principle.

Subrogation is also strong in liability insurance. For example, assume that a washing machine in the insured's place of business catches fire, destroys the insured's building (insured by a policy of property insurance), and also a neighbor's building, thereby creating a liability owed by the insured to the neighbor (which is also covered by a policy of liability insurance). The insurer on both policies pays for the damage to the insured's building and for the neighbor's losses. Upon further investigation, it turns out that a defective motor supplied by a third party within the machine caused the fire. The insurer, as a subrogee under both the property and the liability insurance policies, can assert subrogation rights against the defective motor's manufacturer.

In contrast, because the indemnity principle is weak in life insurance, life insurers do not have subrogation rights when the insured's death is caused by a third party who has legal responsibility for the death. This result is also sometimes explained by the analysis that life insurance is a contract of "investment" rather than "indemnity," and as such it is inappropriate for the insurer to be reimbursed at the expense of beneficiaries, who are entitled to the proceeds of the life insurance policy and who should also own any wrongful death claims arising out of the insured's death. To amplify this point, the assumption is that insurance can never be a dollar-for-dollar replacement for the deceased insured's life, unlike what happens when proceeds are paid under a property insurance policy for the damage to an insured's interest in property. As such, insurance proceeds can never make the beneficiaries "whole," and thus fairness requires that they should also be entitled to recover under any applicable wrongful death claims.

This notion of "wholeness" is also important when evaluating whether the insurer has a right of subrogation. Most courts endorse the general rule, known as the *made-whole rule*, that an insurer is entitled to subrogation only after the insured has been fully compensated for the loss, i.e., has been "made whole." This idea is sometimes expressed under the rubric that the insurer must have paid the debt in full before it is entitled to assert a subrogation right. It can also be understood by reference to the law of suretyship, where a surety remains secondarily liable on a debt until the debt has been fully paid, and thus has no subrogation right while the debt is only partially paid. Indeed, if anything were to be collected from the responsible party, it should first go to the insured if the insured's loss has not been fully reimbursed.

Subrogation is subject to some limitations that may make it unavailable in particular situations. For example, an insurer is not entitled to subrogation against its own insured and is only entitled to subrogation to third parties to whom the insurer owes no duties. The logic seems obvious; if the insurer could subrogate against its own insured, the insurer would be passing its own loss back to its insured—whom it promised to protect with the insurance in the first place. This logic also applies, however, when a co-insured is legally responsible for an injury or damage caused to another co-insured. In that situation, although the law of tort may recognize and enforce a duty running from the party causing the injury to the victim, the fact that they are co-insureds will prevent the insurer who pays for the loss suffered by its insured from pursuing subrogation against a co-insured.

Another limitation emerges from the fact that the insurer-subrogee stands in the shoes of the insured-subrogor for the purpose of asserting subrogation rights. If the tortfeasor-debtor has defenses that are good against the insured, those defenses are also good against the insurer-subrogee asserting subrogation. These defenses might include contributory negligence, laches, a statute of limitations, immunity, a contractual waiver of subrogation rights, or something else. To the extent these defenses are valid, they defeat the insurer's assertion of subrogation rights. A particularly significant potential defense is release; if the insured releases the tortfeasor, the tortfeasor has a perfect defense against the insured who might subsequently sue the tortfeasor, and this same defense is good against the insurer as subrogee. Thus, insurers go to considerable lengths to prevent their insureds from releasing potentially responsible parties, and it is very possible that an insured who releases a tortfeasor will be deemed, under common policy language, to have interfered with the insurer's subrogation rights and thereby forfeited the benefits of coverage. An exception to this analysis is pre-tort releases by insureds of third parties; this is quite common in contracts and business dealings, and while this kind of release may be a valid defense against the insurer's assertion of a subrogation right, it will not ordinarily be deemed to constitute the insured's interference with a subrogation right leading to a forfeiture of coverage.

To summarize, subrogation is an important remedy in the insurance business. Although it serves the purpose of ensuring that losses fall on the legally responsible parties, it also implements the principle of indemnity by preventing insureds from recovering sums more than their losses.[6]

7.3.3 "Other insurance" clauses: coordination of benefits

As discussed above, violating the indemnity principle increases moral hazard. Thus, if multiple policies apply to the same risk or event, which happens frequently, the overlapping coverages can create a situation where the insured has the potential for multiple recoveries under multiple policies, which could result in the insured recovering more than the loss. Thus, almost all property, liability, and health policies, as well as many accident policies, have *other insurance clauses* which seek to prioritize or coordinate the coverage when two or more policies apply to the same loss.

In property insurance where the indemnity principle is strong, the effect of other insurance clauses to prevent windfalls is obvious. In liability insurance, the clauses are directed more at preventing victims from stacking multiple coverages, which has the effect of reducing payments made to a victim of the insured's wrongful behavior. When overlapping policies are coordinated, this reduces the amount of coverage provided in multiple-coverage situations, which theoretically should reduce premiums to the benefit of policyholders. Where the principle of indemnity is weak, as in life insurance, other insurance clauses do not exist. In health insurance, these clauses are very common and are referred to in that setting as *coordination of benefit clauses.*

Insurers use different provisions to coordinate the coverage in overlapping policies. The most common is the pro rata clause, which limits an insurer's liability to a proportion of a loss not exceeding its proportion of the total coverage from all insurers. Another common clause is the excess clause, which provides that the insurer will cover only the loss exceeding other valid and collectible insurance provided by other insurers. The least common is the escape clause, which declares that the insurer has no liability if other insurance is in force on the risk.

A frequent problem is how to enforce the other insurance clauses when the overlapping policies contain different or conflicting clauses. One approach is to attempt to reconcile the clauses through interpretation.

---

6 For more discussion of subrogation, *see* Jerry & Richmond, pp. 560–587.

If reconciliation is not possible or a court is unwilling to attempt it, the likely result is that all the clauses will be declared mutually repugnant and deemed to strike each other out. This approach leaves a gap in the policies regarding coordination that the court must fill in a second phase of the analysis. In this phase, the most common approach is to fill the gap with a pro rata approach, where each insurer pays a share based on the proportion its limit of coverage bears to the total coverage in force. This is essentially the same as converting all clauses in all applicable policies to pro rata clauses. An alternative is to require the insurers to pay equal shares of the loss up to the limits of the policy with the lowest limits; once the limit of the lowest-limit policy is reached, the process is repeated among the remaining policies until the entire loss is covered (a process that necessarily ends when all limits are exhausted). The equal shares approach requires lower-limit insurers to contribute more to a loss than they would under the pro rata approach. However, what commends this approach is that the lowest layers of coverage are the most expensive—because most losses tend to be smaller. Thus, as an actuarial matter, a larger share of a premium should be allocated to smaller losses, which arguably makes it fairer to require insurers with overlapping coverages to contribute to losses under the equal shares formula.

To summarize, it is common for multiple policies to apply to the same occurrence or loss. The indemnity principle can be implicated by these overlapping coverages, and insurers seek to limit their exposures through clauses that coordinate coverage when other insurance is present.[7]

---

[7] For more discussion of other insurance clauses, *see* Douglas R. Richmond, *Issues and Problems in "Other Insurance," Multiple Insurance, and Self-Insurance*, 22 PEPP. L. REV. 1373 (1995); JERRY & RICHMOND, pp. 588–612.

8 Insurance as agreement: the influence of contract law

As discussed in Chapter 3, insurance is usually conceptualized as a contract—a binding agreement that serves risk-transference and risk-distribution functions. Even public regulators, accustomed to thinking of the insurance business as a regulated industry, begin with the premise, sometimes stated in a statute or code,[1] that insurance is a contract between a policyholder and an insurer. Because insurance law has evolved within the larger context of contract law, it should come as no surprise that general contract law principles have been very influential in determining the meaning of policies and the scope of the parties' rights and obligations. Also, because insurance is a special kind of contract, it should come as no surprise that contract doctrines have often been stretched and pulled when applied to insurance transactions.

8.1 Reasonable expectations

Contract law is the law of promissory obligation, and thus one of its purposes—and arguably its primary purpose—is to protect expectations induced by promises.[2] Whether this purpose is based on enforcing a moral

---

1 *See*, e.g., [ITALY] ART. 1882 CIVIL CODE ("Insurance is the contract with which the insurer ... obliged himself ..."); [SPAIN] ART. 1 INSURANCE CONTRACT ACT (referring to insurance as a contract); [US] FLA. STAT. § 624.02 ("Insurance" is a contract whereby one undertakes to indemnify ...").

2 *See* ARTHUR L. CORBIN, CORBIN ON CONTRACTS, § 1 (1963) ("The main purpose of contract law is the realization of reasonable expectations induced by promises"). The *Principles on European Contract Law*, Art. 1:102, frame

duty to keep promises, promoting efficient investment and exchange in markets, encouraging cooperative activities, or something else, the basic idea is that when promises are voluntarily exchanged thereby creating an expectation of benefit, or when a promise is made that foreseeably induces the promisee's reliance, the law should give a remedy to the promisee if the promise is not performed, subject to rules that adapt this proposition to the diverse situations that arise in complex markets and relationships. This core purpose is often cast as protecting the reasonable expectations of the promisee, which recognizes the possibility that a promisee might acquire or claim rights so unreasonable that enforcing them would be unfair to the promisor. This purpose applies with equal force across all fields of law with roots in contract law, such as labor and employment law, agency law, real estate law, and insurance law. Thus, whenever policyholders seek to enforce insurance policies, or insurers seek to deny the existence of obligations under them, the rules of contract law designed to protect the reasonable expectations of a promisee are in play. Yet, as discussed in Chapter 3, the importance of insurance as a security-creating tool has caused special characteristics to be ascribed to insurance policies, which has led to insurance policies frequently being treated as a "special" kind of contract. This specialness has manifested itself in some jurisdictions in the US in the form of a supercharged view of what it means to protect reasonable expectations when insurance contracts are involved.

The role that standardization of consumer contracts plays in this narrative should not be underestimated. In a famous 1943 article, Friedrich Kessler used insurance to illustrate his thesis about standardization and adhesion, as he worked his way toward an explanation of reasonable expectations:

> In dealing with standardized contracts courts have to determine what the weaker contract party could legitimately expect by way of services according to the enterpriser's "calling," and to what extent the stronger party disappointed reasonable expectations based on the typical life situation.[3]

---

expectations in terms of the parties' freedom to set contract terms: "Parties are free to enter into a contract and to determine its contents, subject to the requirements of good faith and fair dealing, and the mandatory rules established by these Principles."

3 Friedrich Kessler, *Contracts of Adhesion—Some Thoughts about Freedom of Contract*, 43 Colum. L. Rev. 629, 634–637 (1943).

Spencer Kimball took this a step further 17 years later when he identified "reasonable expectations" as a "principle" that limits the ability of insurers in some situations to draft explicit language negating coverage.[4] In Kimball's formulation, "reasonable expectations" becomes a limiting principle that imposes a substantive limit on the agreement that an insurer and policyholder can reach—or more accurately, on what terms the insurer can draft, market, sell, and then enforce against a policyholder. This understanding of "reasonable expectations" goes well beyond the original contract law principle.

Ten years after Kimball's insight, Robert Keeton authored a two-part article[5] in which he observed that it was exceedingly difficult, if not impossible, to reconcile the outcomes in many insurance law cases with the traditional contract doctrines ostensibly being used to reach those results. His point was that contract law principles as deployed in insurance cases had broken away from the traditional contract law understandings. He suggested two principles anchored the insurance law cases, the second of which was that "the objectively reasonable expectations of applicants and intended beneficiaries regarding the terms of insurance contracts will be honored even though painstaking study of the policy provisions would have negated those expectations."[6] Under this formulation, reasonable expectations of a policyholder existing extraneously to the text of the writing, if objectively reasonable, will be enforced even if the text of the policy—which presumably accurately reflects the insurer's expectations—is inconsistent with the policyholder's expectations.

Since Keeton's 1970 articles, this aptly named *doctrine of reasonable expectations* has had a mixed reception. Some courts embraced it, others rejected it, and some that embraced it later recanted their earlier position. Some observers criticized the doctrine as amounting to judicially created coverage,[7] while others applauded it as representing an appropriate

---

4 *See* Spencer L. Kimball, Insurance and Public Policy, pp. 210–211, 224 (1960).

5 Robert E. Keeton, *Insurance Law Rights at Variance with Policy Provisions: Part One*, 83 Harv. L. Rev. 961 (1970); Robert E. Keeton, *Insurance Law Rights at Variance with Policy Provisions: Part Two*, 83 Harv. L. Rev. 1281 (1970).

6 83 Harv. L. Rev. at 967.

7 *See*, e.g., Stephen J. Ware, *A Critique of the Reasonable Expectations Doctrine*, 56 U. Chi. L. Rev. 1461 (1989); *Gregorio v. GEICO Gen. Ins. Co.*,

re-balancing of the power differential between policyholder and insurance company.[8] Others suggested that the doctrine simply amounted to a ramping up of other well-established principles by, for example, relieving claimants from certain evidentiary obligations.[9]

Thus, what began as a foundational principle in contract law—protecting the reasonable expectations of contracting parties created by the contract—evolved in some jurisdictions to impose duties on insurance companies not found in the agreement itself. From the insurance company perspective, this evolution amounted to a weaponization of the contract law principle and the destruction of the reliability of contract text. From the policyholder's perspective, this evolution constituted an additional step toward fairness in a situation where one party controls the forms, the other receives the form on a take-it-or-leave-it basis, and the drafter should understand, and thus can be fairly bound to, the expectations this form creates in its recipient. In short, with respect to reasonable expectations, insurance law reflects the core value of contract law, but many courts and commentators have given reasonable expectations a more expansive meaning in insurance law.

8.2 Interpretation

For as long as the law has enforced agreements, contracting parties have often disputed the answers to two questions: first, what are the terms of

---

815 F.Supp.2d 1097, 1100 (D. Ariz. 2011) ("courts cannot invoke the doctrine [of reasonable expectations] to create a new bargain without any basis in the written terms of the agreement").

8 *See*, e.g., Roger C. Henderson, *The Doctrine of Reasonable Expectations in Insurance Law after Two Decades*, 51 Ohio St. L. J. 823, 853 (1990) (the doctrine "balances the needs of insureds against those of insurers, as it continues to further the overriding goal of fair and equitable allocation of costs of accidents and sickness").

9 To explain, the law of misrepresentation ordinarily requires the plaintiff to prove reliance on the misrepresentation. Under the doctrine of reasonable expectations, a plaintiff who established that a misrepresentation created a reasonable expectation of coverage would not need to prove reliance to enforce that expectation. For more discussion, *see* Kenneth S. Abraham, *Judge-Made Law and Judge-Made Insurance: Honoring the Reasonable Expectations of the Insured*, 67 Va. L. Rev. 1151 (1981).

the agreement; and second, what do the terms mean. Insurance companies invest heavily in drafting elaborate forms that are intended to reflect—and will usually state explicitly that they do reflect—the entire agreement of the parties, and that there are no agreements, oral or written, outside the writing. Thus, in insurance transactions, it is rare for insurer and policyholder to disagree about whether particular terms were agreed upon and were then left out of the writing. When this issue arises, it usually involves a policyholder's allegation that a written endorsement or rider was inadvertently omitted from a policy, a mistake was made in the description of what is being insured or the limits of the coverage, or an included coverage was deleted during the process of policy renewal.

The more likely dispute in insurance transactions involves the second question. A dispute over meaning can arise when the parties at the time of contracting each subjectively attach different meanings to a term or provision, but it can also arise when one party for strategic advantage claims after the contract was formed that a contract term means something different from what the parties understood the term to mean at the time of contracting.

In contract law generally, the interpretive principles and approaches that can be applied vary, with consequences for results. What is sometimes labeled as the *contextual approach* seeks to identify the meaning attached to a contested term by inquiring into any relevant extrinsic evidence that sheds light on what each party knew or should have reasonably known about what the term meant, including what each party knew or should have known about the other party's understanding. Written texts and other words used by the parties matter, but what is paramount is determining what the parties intended from all relevant circumstances. Thus, the contextual approach allows for the possibility that the parties jointly selected a meaning that departs from the customary meaning of text as understood by authors of dictionaries and other reasonable third parties. Ordinarily, the result will favor the understanding of the party who had less knowledge about or reason to know the meaning attached to the term by the other party.

The contextual approach, by diminishing the importance of a writing relative to other extrinsic evidence, creates opportunities for parties to engage in strategic behavior by asserting meanings at odds with what an objective reader might say is plain on the face of a writing. Thus, this lack of respect for the objective meanings of words has led many courts to follow a different approach, which is commonly called the *plain meaning rule*. Applying the plain meaning rule is essentially a two-step process. If one party asserts that a term is ambiguous, the court will initially inquire into whether the term has a plain meaning—and if it does, this plain meaning controls. In contrast to the contextual approach, one party's assertion of ambiguity is not enough under plain meaning analysis to trigger examination of extrinsic evidence. Only if the court as a matter of law upon examination of the writing[10] finds the existence of an ambiguity will extrinsic evidence be considered to determine meaning. This means that plain meaning, if it exists, controls—and the party asserting that plain meaning prevails. The critique of this approach, beyond the obvious point that plain meaning has the potential to disregard what the parties actually intended, is that whenever a court considers whether an ambiguity exists on the face of a writing, the court is, in fact, making use of extrinsic evidence. The judge is referring to the judge's own life experiences, perhaps reading dictionaries, and referencing how the term is used in a particular trade or in society generally, and that this extrinsic evidence should not be elevated in importance above extrinsic evidence that the parties themselves would offer. One way to state the difference between these two approaches is that the plain meaning approach reduces the range of extrinsic evidence that can be considered in determining whether an ambiguity exists. Once an ambiguity is found, however, the approaches merge and allow the consideration of all relevant evidence.

The tension between contextual and plain meaning interpretation exists in insurance law.[11] Policyholders disappointed about insurers' denials of coverage often argue that they attached a particular meaning to terms, sometimes with the encouragement of agents or brokers with authority to represent the insurer, and that this understanding of a policy's meaning should control. The policyholder perspective is that public policy requires

---

10 This can happen with oral agreements, too. However, if an agreement is not in writing, each party is likely to be alleging a particular term that is different from the term the other party is alleging—and the question before the fact-finder is to determine what the term of the agreement is, as opposed to what the agreed-upon term means.

11 For more discussion of different approaches to contract interpretation and how they relate to reasonable expectations, *see* Peter N. Swisher, *A Realistic Consensus Approach to the Insurance Law Doctrine of Reasonable Expectations*, 35 Tort & Ins. L. J. 729 (2000).

that policies conform to the reasonable understandings consumers have about the scope of coverage—understandings that sophisticated drafters should know insureds possess and that they should specifically and clearly negate if coverage is not intended. In contrast, insurers, having invested much in the drafting of standardized forms, are highly motivated to defend the written policies and argue that the language used in the texts has plain meanings that should be enforced. Insurers argue that unless the forms are interpreted and enforced according to their plain meanings (i.e., how the insurers intended them), the assumptions underlying pricing, underwriting, and fair claims management will no longer be reliable.

In both approaches, courts use a variety of axioms to determine meaning when ambiguity is found. One of the most important interprets ambiguous language against the drafter, under the reasoning that the drafter controls the form and thus is in the best position to avoid ambiguities. When applied in insurance when standardized forms are used, this rule, which is called *contra proferentem*, invariably favors policyholders. Another axiom frequently used in insurance cases is a specific application of *contra proferentem*: coverage provisions are interpreted broadly, and exclusions are interpreted narrowly. A variety of other axioms are used in contract law generally and insurance law specifically, such as an express reference to one matter excludes other matters, a specific reference controls the general when the two are in conflict, and a general reference at the end of a series of specific references is limited by the class formed by the specific references.

Interpretation is itself a form of judicial regulation of the insurance contract; decisions in adjudicated cases can serve as a precedent to determine the scope of coverage in future cases, and insurers sometimes respond to decisions expanding coverage beyond what they intended to provide by narrowing the coverage sold in future policies. Standardization of forms, however, complicates the situation, as insurers that sell forms across jurisdictional boundaries may not wish to modify a form to account for one negative interpretation in one locale, especially since any change in coverage must be evaluated against the pricing and underwriting standards for sale of the policy which were set with the existing coverage in mind. In addition, an insurer that subscribes to a form sold to an association of insurers is likely to be deterred from customizing the form for its own use, as then the insurer loses the benefit of the data that supports the form—which is why the insurer did not use its own form in the first place.

Not surprisingly, the use of standardized forms puts pressure on contract law's interpretive principles because consumers typically do not read and have no desire to understand such forms—and thus it makes little sense to try to discern a policyholder's expectations with respect to the content of a standardized form. Although the same point could be made about other kinds of consumer contracts, the security-enhancing and risk-management purposes of insurance contracts are arguably so uniquely important to the public interest that "insurance-policy-interpretation rules are properly to be considered to be distinct from general contract-interpretation rules in some respects."[12]

8.3 Misrepresentation (and breach of warranty)

In general contract law, once the requirements for creating an enforceable contract are met, the law recognizes circumstances that, when present, render the apparent contract unenforceable. These circumstances include unilateral and mutual mistakes, illegality, and agreements offending public policy by, for example, impairing family relationships, unreasonably restraining trade, inducing violations of fiduciary duties, and unreasonably interfering with other contractual relationships.

One of the most important rules in this category is *misrepresentation.* A misrepresentation is essentially an assertion that is not in accord with the facts; in some circumstances, a concealment or a non-disclosure is treated as the equivalent of a misrepresentation. In general contract law,

---

12 RESTATEMENT OF THE LAW—LIABILITY INSURANCE, § 2 *com.* h (2018). For more discussion about insurance contract interpretation, *see* Jeffrey W. Stempel, *What is the Meaning of "Plain Meaning"?*, 56 TORT TRIAL & INS. PRAC. L. J. 551 (2021); Kenneth S. Abraham, *Plain Meaning, Extrinsic Evidence, and Ambiguity: Myth and Reality in Insurance Policy Interpretation*, 25 CONN. INS. L. J. 329 (2019); Kenneth S. Abraham, *A Theory of Insurance Policy Interpretation*, 95 MICH. L. REV. 531 (1996); Mark A. Geistfeld, *Interpreting the Rules of Insurance Contract Interpretation*, 68 RUTGERS U. L. REV. 371 (2015); JERRY & RICHMOND, pp. 117–127; Swisher, *supra* n. 11.

a party to a contract can void it if that party's manifestation of assent was induced by either a fraudulent or material misrepresentation upon which that party justifiably relied. This rule is sometimes explained, with some circularity, as an application of the mutual assent requirement: if a party receives and relies upon false information provided by the other party when deciding to enter into an agreement, the recipient's expression of assent is defective, which means that mutual assent never actually existed.[13] The better explanation is that efficient markets, which contract law supports, depend upon full, free, and accurate information. Market participants should not be encouraged to circulate false information that induces recipients to enter into agreements they would not have sought had they known the truth, or to allocate resources differently than they would have if they possessed accurate information. Thus, those who engage in these deceptive behaviors should not be allowed to enforce the deals their false representations induce.

The law of misrepresentation is especially important in insurance law because of how insurance companies use applications when selling their products. When an applicant seeks coverage and the insurer is evaluating whether to provide it and at what price, the insurer needs information about the applicant and the risk proposed to be covered, and the process of acquiring that information has a cost. Obviously, it would be cost prohibitive for an insurer to investigate every relevant detail of every applicant and their proposed risks. Insurers deal with this challenge by asking applicants to provide information in written form and affirm its validity, and then relying on this applicant-provided information. If the policy is issued and a claim is submitted, the insurer relies on the law of misrepresentation to deny the claim if it is determined at that time that information provided in the application was false. Thus, insurers depend

13 Note that this same logic applies to coercion and duress, and the party who makes a contract under conditions of coercion or duress is entitled to void it. Also under this principle, a party's manifestation of assent could be rendered defective by false or inaccurate information supplied by a party outside the transaction. In such a situation, giving the recipient the ability to void the contract could be unfair to the other party if the other party had nothing to do with creating or transmitting the false information. The law deals with this problem through an exception that takes away the recipient's power to void the contract if the other party to the agreement, without reason to know of the misrepresentation and in good faith, relies materially on the existence of the agreement, such as by giving value to the other party.

on the defense of misrepresentation to reduce the costs of information gathering in the underwriting process.

Insurers also rely on the misrepresentation defense to maintain the integrity of their risk pools, which is fundamental to the reliability of insurance contracts. Of course, policyholders who submit accurate information on their applications that fail to meet the insurer's underwriting standards are rejected and kept out of the risk pools. If an applicant submits false information on the application and is admitted to the risk pool, and if the applicant suffers no loss during the policy term, the insurer collects the premium and the risk pool is not harmed. If, however, the misrepresenting applicant suffers a loss, the insurer during claims processing will hopefully discover the misrepresentation and will use it as a defense against the claim, thereby protecting the integrity of the risk pool.

Misrepresentation can also be used abusively by insurers to deny valid claims, and part of insurance law involves the appearance and evolution of rules to address these unfair practices. For example, a practice developed early in the twentieth century where some life insurers would deny beneficiaries' claims based on alleged misrepresentations, essentially challenging them to bring an action on the policy where they would bear the difficult burden of proving that the deceased policyholder did not commit a misrepresentation. In some jurisdictions, statutes and regulations were created that create a time period (such as two years) after which the policy becomes incontestable if the misrepresentation defense has not been raised already. In some jurisdictions, laws require that a misrepresentation has a causal relationship to the loss, which narrows the potential reach of the defense. Under these laws, the misrepresentation might have been relevant to the insurer's underwriting decision, but if the misrepresented fact is not causally related to the loss in question, the insurer is not allowed to assert it as a reason to deny the claim.[14]

Closely related to the misrepresentation defense is a quaint relic of the maritime era (i.e., the 1500s and 1600s) when those underwriting risk would require those seeking insurance to "warrant" certain characteristics of the vessel and the voyage, such as how many guns and sailors would be on board, when the vessel would sail, etc. As the law of *warranty* in

---

14 For more discussion of the misrepresentation defense and the closely related concealment defense, *see* JERRY & RICHMOND, pp. 641–663.

insurance developed, the insurer would have a valid defense to coverage if the warranty were not strictly satisfied, which departed from the misrepresentation rule that a defense existed only if the false statement were a substantial deviation from the true facts and was materially related to the risk. Insurer exuberance in the use of warranties led to their regulation—so much so that warranties in insurance law today are functionally equivalent to representations. Some of the overreach through warranties was so substantial that courts created odd rules to regulate them. For example, the rule emerged that unless a warranty was explicitly written as a promise about future conditions, the warranty would be interpreted as an *affirmative warranty*, which means that the warranty only represents a state of facts prevailing at the time the policy was issued. Thus, if the policyholder purchasing fire insurance represented that the insured building had a functioning sprinkler system (which was the situation when the policy was issued), the insurer could not use the fact that the system was not working at the time of the fire as a basis for denying the claim.

Interestingly, the strict regulation of warranty has led most insurers to draft their policies with the language of coverage rather than warranty. In the foregoing example, today the policy would likely be drafted as "no coverage exists if at the time of the fire the sprinkler system is not functional." The intent of the language is the same, but the coverage formulation is arguably superior in that the consequences of not having a functional sprinkler system are clearer than if the policyholder "warrants" such a system. Thus, the regulation of warranties may not have changed the scope of coverage provided to policyholders, but it has arguably made policies clearer.[15]

8.4 Waiver and estoppel

In contract law, the term *waiver* is usually used to refer to the voluntary and intentional relinquishment of a known right; as such, a waiver can arise in a variety of situations. Waiver is frequently used to explain what happens when a promisor with a conditional duty announces that he will

15 For more discussion of the warranty defense, *see* JERRY & RICHMOND, pp. 624–641.

perform despite the non-occurrence of the condition; the non-occurrence would entitle the promisor to suspend performance (and eventually treat the duty as discharged), but the waiver excuses the non-occurrence of the condition, thereby preserving the promisee's entitlement to the performance. Waivers are often express, but they can also be implied from the circumstances.

The term *estoppel* refers to a legal principle that prevents someone from making an argument or asserting a right because of one's previous words or actions to the contrary. The logic of the principle is that one's words or behavior can induce reliance by or create an expectation in someone else, such that it prejudices that other party if the speaker or actor were allowed to make the argument or assert the right in question.

In insurance law, the doctrines of waiver and estoppel are powerful workhorses—largely because the contours of these doctrines are imprecise and malleable, allowing courts to invoke these doctrines to explain outcomes that seem just in the circumstances. For example, a court might recognize a waiver to prevent an insurer from asserting an exclusion to coverage if the insurer failed to mention it in the first communication with the policyholder, enforcing a deadline for some act required of the insured if the insurer did not mention it when it had an opportunity to do so, or enforcing a condition to coverage if the insurer accepted a premium payment with knowledge that the insured was out of compliance with the condition. Insurers have been estopped to deny the validity of coverage when they induced an insured not to purchase alternative coverage by misrepresenting that existing insurance was valid, delivered a policy form to the policyholder (thereby signifying that the coverage was effective) despite knowledge of the insured's material misrepresentation, or represented to the insured that premiums were fully paid even though they were not (thereby estopping the insurer to cancel the policy for nonpayment of premiums).[16]

---

16 For more discussion of waiver and estoppel, *see* JERRY & RICHMOND, pp. 134–145.

8.5 Remedies for nonperformance

The overarching principle that describes contract remedies is that the aggrieved promisee should be put in as good a position as the promisee would have occupied if the contract had been performed. The obvious logic of this principle is that a remedy of this magnitude is needed to protect expectations. Measuring damages in terms of the aggrieved party's reliance interest—i.e., restoring the aggrieved party to the position occupied before the contract was made—does not protect expectation and is thus a suboptimal remedy. Indeed, in insurance, only compensating an aggrieved policyholder's reliance interest would merely return the previously paid premium to the insured, which would fail completely to provide the security that the insured sought when purchasing the policy.

Insurance law begins with contract law's premise of securing expectations, but because what is sold in an insurance contract is security from risk, the remedies available in insurance law sometimes go beyond what contract law would allow. Using a contract damages formula, if an insurer breaches its duty to pay the insured's covered loss, the insurer must pay the amount of proceeds required by the contract.[17] If an insurer breaches its duty to defend under a liability policy, the insurer must reimburse the costs the insured incurred to secure its own defense. The conceptual problem, however, is that the insured purchased security against the prospect of a future loss, and the insurer's nonperformance eviscerates the essence of what the insured purchased. To illustrate, a party who is aggrieved by the seller's failure to deliver beans can go into the market, buy substitute beans, and then receive compensation equal to the difference between the cost of the substitute beans and the contract price, plus additional expenses required to execute the substitute transaction. But when a policyholder buys security and the insurer does not deliver it, the insured endures exactly what the insured feared—the suffering of an unprotected loss. The insured might file a lawsuit and pursue and obtain

---

17 In the common law, this is technically a substitution remedy based on the loss in value of the insurer's performance—and not an order to the insurer to specifically perform its contract duty. In the civil law, which is more receptive to specific performance remedies, the remedy is more likely to be an order that the insurer perform its contract duty. In either case, the remedy accomplishes the same result.

a remedy, but this does not deliver the security that the insured expected when the loss occurred.

Further, what distinguishes insurance from the sale of beans is that contract remedies, by themselves, give the insurer little reason not to breach. The damages charged to the defaulting seller will be a function of the price at which the buyer purchases substitute beans; this price is theoretically unlimited, which means the seller's theoretical damages are infinite. If the insurer promises to pay proceeds, the most that contract law will require the insurer to pay is the amount of proceeds—which means that the insurer has little to lose by declining to perform. Indeed, withholding performance may enable the insurer to assert power over a desperate insured who needs proceeds quickly to avoid other devastating consequences. The liability insurer which breaches the duty to defend will probably pay under contract law's damage measure slightly more in attorneys' fees than if the insurer had provided a defense (the attorney selected by the insured will probably be more expensive than the attorney the insurer would have appointed), but this measure does little to deter the insurer from testing coverage since the remedy, under contract law, will be no more than what the insurer's performance would have entailed anyway.

Courts and sometimes legislatures have responded to the limitations of traditional contract remedies in the insurance setting by devising ways to impose what are essentially extracontractual damages for some kinds of insurer breaches. For example, when the insurer's breach is deemed to involve bad faith (which fits most circumstances where the insurer's breach is strategic), extracontractual damages are sometimes awarded. Statutes in some US states require insurers to pay statutory penalties to insureds when the insurer is found to have failed to perform its duties, or to pay the insured's attorneys' fees (which is a shift of the prevailing parties' obligation in the US to bear their own attorneys' fees). Although a judgment above policy limits is a foreseeable consequence of an insurer's breach of the duty to settle in liability insurance and thus should be recoverable under contract law doctrine, some courts have explained the insurer's duty to settle as sounding in tort, which opens up the possibility of a broader range of consequential damages (such as emotional distress, which is rarely awarded as a contract remedy).

In short, remedies in insurance law draw heavily from the principles of contract law, but in keeping with the observation that insurance policies are special kinds of contracts, the range of damages awarded to policy-holders aggrieved by insurer breaches often go beyond what contract law would allow.

9 Scope of coverage: the boundaries of the insurer's obligation

The extent to which an insurer provides coverage is based on the insurer's assessment of the risk it assumes. This is a multi-faceted analysis which includes evaluations of the magnitude of the peril, the frequency of loss and projected frequency of claims, the insurer's ability to distribute the risk in reliable and manageable pools, the forecasted expenses of claims processing, and competitive pressures in the marketplace where the product is sold. When the actuarial analysis is completed and the drafters finish their work, the policy's coverage will be a bounded description of coverage. Much insurance law has been created when courts resolve disputes between policyholders and insurers over the location of these boundaries, which separate covered from non-covered losses.

The insurance world is far too vast to examine even a small proportion of common coverage problems here. To provide a taste of the subject of scope of coverage, this chapter discusses three representative and recurring issues, each of which illustrates the interesting dynamics involved in determining the boundaries of insurance coverage.

9.1 Policy text: boundaries described by words and phrases

One of the most important tools insurers use to delineate coverage is through definitions. Yet despite the intense effort and expense insurers commit to drafting precise definitions, anticipating all circumstances that might implicate a definition is impossible. Even terms with seemingly clear meanings can fail to account for unusual situations at the margin.

To illustrate, consider a Utah (US) case[1] where the accidental death policy excluded coverage for death resulting from the use of a "device for aerial navigation." The insured died in an accident involving a water ski kite, and the insurer denied coverage on the ground that this activity fell within the exclusion. On the one hand, a device (like a water ski kite) tethered to the ground (or in this case, a boat), which uses the wind to stay aloft and depends for its safe operation on the tether remaining secure, does not seem to be a device that "navigates" the airspace like a plane, parachute, or hang glider, where the pilot or operator controls the device's direction, speed, altitude, and where and when it lands. On the other hand, the passenger on a water ski kite being towed by a boat has some, albeit limited, control over altitude and direction. The insurer's purpose was to exclude death resulting from travel in the air, but the words it chose—"aerial navigation"—were unclear when applied to an aerial device capable of only limited control by its passenger.

To take another example, most policies in every line of insurance contain an exclusion for losses occurring because of "war."[2] This is because war has the potential to result in widespread destruction on a massive scale, and, as discussed in Chapters 2 and 11, insurers vigorously avoid insuring correlated risks. Also, war cannot be predicted by using actuarial tables. Yet in many situations, whether a war has occurred requires a more detailed analysis than the word "war" standing alone provides. The first war exclusions date back to the 1700s when the effects of war on maritime trade became a concern for insurers, but war in that era—hostile armed conflict between sovereign nations—was a relatively unambiguous state of affairs. When civilian targets were bombed from long distance in the Spanish Civil War (1936–39), which happened as increased militarism, uprisings, and violent revolts were occurring on the continent, insurers took notice that the war exclusions then in use were not sufficient to exclude all situations where war-like damage could occur. This led the

---

1 *Oeschler v. Fireman's Fund Am. Life Ins. Co.*, 663 P. 2d 97 (Utah 1983) (3-2 decision holding that a water ski kite is a "device for aerial navigation," and thus the insured's death, which occurred when the tow rope disengaged and the insured crashed on land, was not covered under the accidental death policy).

2 Some, but not all, life insurance and workers compensation policies lack war exclusions.

London market in 1938 to introduce a standard-form war exclusion (known as "NMA 464") which applied to loss or damage resulting from:

> war, invasion, acts of foreign enemies, hostilities (whether war be declared or not), civil war, rebellion, revolution, insurrection, military or usurped power, or confiscation or nationalization or requisition or destruction of or damage to property by or under the order of any government or public or local authority.[3]

This modification added scope to the exclusion by including many kinds of war-like violence previously not understood as "war," but this modification did not anticipate the prospect of—and did not unambiguously address—terrorist acts by non-sovereign entities, like those which destroyed the World Trade Center towers and part of the Pentagon in the US on September 11, 2001. As one would expect, insurers and reinsurers moved quickly to exclude terrorism coverage from most coverages after 9/11.[4] Indeed, questions about the scope of the modern war exclusions are under active discussion today. For example, is loss suffered during a "peacekeeping mission" within the war exclusion? "Insurrection" is listed in the typical war exclusion; was the assault on the US Capitol on January 6, 2022, an "insurrection"? Are state-sponsored cyberattacks "hostile or warlike acts" within the meaning of war exclusions, accepting that they do not involve traditional warfare tactics, but "traditional" is not a word found in standard exclusions?

In short, even the most precise definitions and drafting that seem clear in one setting will be challenged—and might fail—when the language is applied in new circumstances. One of the most prominent illustrations of this phenomenon in modern times occurred because of the COVID-19 pandemic. The insuring agreement in most standard property insurance policies contains the insurer's promise to pay for "direct physical loss or

---

3 *See* Javier C. Malagon, *What Does Insurance Cover During a War? A Journey through History*, Mapfre (Feb. 3, 2022), https://www.mapfre.com/en/insights/insurance/what-does-insurance-cover-during-a-war.

4 The resulting unavailability of coverage was an economic crisis in many countries, and many governments enacted backstops (such as caps on industry-wide liabilities, at which point government becomes the underwriter) and publicly funded reinsurance schemes to stabilize the insurance industry and meet the demand for coverage. For more information, *see* OECD, *Terrorism Risk Insurance Programmes by Country* (undated), https://www.oecd.org/daf/fin/insurance/terrorism-risk-insurance-programmes.htm.

damage" to covered property caused by covered perils. For destruction of or damage to property due to perils such as fire or weather, or for the physical dispossession of property due to perils such as theft or conversion, this language works well in most situations. Business policyholders also desire to purchase coverage for income lost due to business interruptions when property cannot be used while it is damaged or lost and in the process of being repaired or replaced. Thus, when insurers extended property insurance to cover insureds' loss of use of the property (i.e., the time value of property, as distinct from the intrinsic value of property), insurers carried forward in most policies the triggering language requiring a "direct physical loss or damage."

COVID-19's appearance in early 2020 and the global pandemic that followed represented a major unanticipated change in the environment in which this policy language was applied. Government shutdown orders shuttered many business locations, business activities were interrupted, and income was lost on a massive scale. Many policyholders sought proceeds under their business interruption policies, but they encountered insurers' arguments that COVID-19 caused no "direct, physical loss" of property. Insurers argued that COVID-19 existed in the air and on surfaces but caused no physical damage to property on which it landed or surrounded. Policyholders argued that being unable to use property because of government shutdown orders issued due to the presence of the virus constituted a "physical loss" because policyholders were not allowed to make physical, active use of property, and this denial of access constituted a "loss" of property. As of 2022, these cases are the subject of widespread litigation, and thus far represent the most intensely litigated insurance law issue arising out of the pandemic.[5]

The nub of the problem is that until 2020, insurers and policyholders did not have significant shared experiences with pandemics. The setting in which modern property insurance forms were designed, sold, and administered did not contemplate an environment where business inter-

---

5 In the US, insurers have won most of these cases. *See* Penn Law, *Covid Coverage Litigation Tracker*, https://cclt.law.upenn.edu/. In the UK, a coverage test case was decided in 2021 mostly in favor of insureds and claims are now being processed. *See* Financial Conduct Authority (UK), *Business Interruption Insurance* (Aug. 12, 2022), https://www.fca.org.uk/firms/business-interruption-insurance.

ruption would occur on a global scale due to a virus or a bacterium. This may stand as the most powerful illustration in this century of how policy language drafted in one setting can be challenged when supervening circumstances create an unfamiliar environment in which the language is applied.[6]

9.2 Intentionally caused loss and the meaning of "accident"

The fundamental assumption that a loss must be fortuitous or accidental in some sense to be eligible for coverage was discussed in Chapter 7. It should follow that intentionally caused losses are not covered, but it turns out that this generalization is only correct to a point—thereby setting up one of the most interesting coverage boundaries in insurance law.

9.2.1 First-party insurance: life, accidental death, and property insurance

In life insurance, intentional self-destruction, i.e., suicide, is a clear example of a policyholder who owns the interest in the subject of the insurance (i.e., who insures one's own life) intentionally causing the loss. Yet life insurance is commonly purchased for the benefit of third parties, i.e., the designated beneficiaries, and from the perspective of these persons, the policyholder's intentional self-destruction is unexpected and accidental. Thus, the rule followed in almost all jurisdictions is that suicide does not preclude coverage under a life insurance policy, and no *general* exclusion exists in life insurance eliminating such coverage when it occurs. However, the concern that life insurance might be purchased for the purpose of enriching beneficiaries through suicide—an adverse selection concern[7]—causes most life insurance policies to contain a narrow exclusion for suicide that occurs within a set period (usually one to three

---

6 For more discussion, *see* Steve Browning, *Coronavirus: Business Interruption Insurance*, House of Commons Library (Nov. 19, 2021), https://commonslibrary.parliament.uk/research-briefings/cbp-8917/; Christopher C. French, *COVID-19 Business Interruption Insurance Losses: The Cases For and Against Coverage*, 27 Conn. Ins. L. J. 1 (2020).

7 Adverse selection is discussed in Chapter 2.

years) after a policy is issued. Except for this exclusion designed to address adverse selection, nothing renders intentional acts of self-destruction uninsurable.

With respect to accidental death insurance, however, suicide has different implications. In this type of policy, the insuring agreement typically references a sudden or unexpected event, outside the control of the policyholder, involving some kind of special force or impact. Under this language, suicide is not an accident, and benefits are not paid to beneficiaries under accidental death policies when the insured intentionally takes their own life. Yet this seemingly straightforward answer disguises some difficult questions. If an insured were insane at the time of the suicide, does this negate the intent to cause one's own death and thereby render the death accidental? Beneficiaries would frequently argue that it did, and sometimes the fact of suicide was offered as evidence of the insured's insanity. Courts and juries sometimes sided with the beneficiaries, and insurers settled many of these cases rather than put the question to a jury. This has caused most modern accidental death policies to exclude coverage for suicide "whether sane or insane," thereby drawing a boundary around intentional acts that prevents an inquiry into the policyholder's state of mind.

But what if an insured accidentally suffers a head trauma that produces a mental condition under which the insured succumbs to an "irresistible impulse" to take one's own life? Or what if an insured's prescription medicine directly leads to depression that causes the insured to commit suicide? Although most courts reason that it is not necessary for the insured to understand the implications of their acts or to form a conscious purpose to commit an act of self-destruction, and that it is only necessary that the insured intends the action that leads to death, some courts reason that intent does not exist if the insured lacks control over the mental processes used to form intent.

The challenges with defining the scope of coverage do not end here. What if the insured intentionally engages in an act that is likely, but not certain, to lead to one's own death? Is that conduct accidental? And at what point is something "likely" to occur? In a Florida case, an insured, despondent over the breakup of his marriage, played "Russian roulette" and died; the court held that intentionally engaging in a game with a one-in-six probability of fatal consequences was not accidental.[8] Typically, those who drive while intoxicated do not intend to bring about their own deaths, but cognizant of the fact that driving while intoxicated is extremely hazardous and the act of getting behind the wheel of a vehicle in that condition is intentional, most courts have held that policyholders' deaths in motor vehicle accidents attributable to their intoxication are not accidents for the purposes of accidental death benefits.[9] Another line of cases involves individuals who use illegal drugs (such as heroin or cocaine) and die as a result. Under the view of some courts, the insured does not "intend" one's own death; indeed, in most situations, the insured probably used illegal drugs before without a negative consequence. For other courts, the dangers of illegal drugs are so well known that death after using such a drug is not an accident.[10]

To summarize this landscape in accidental death insurance, at one extreme, the insured who stumbles into traffic and is killed has died in an accident. At the other extreme, the insured who deliberately lays down in front of a speeding train has committed suicide. It is the grey area between the two extremes—for example, where the insured recklessly plays "chicken" with a speeding train without intending to die—that presents the difficulties. Insurers favor narrow constructions of coverage, and those policyholders who do not engage in this behavior should agree, as they should not want their premiums to be used to subsidize those who assume these risks (and raise the costs of the pool, with consequences for everyone in it). But beneficiaries submitting claims for proceeds naturally favor broad interpretations of the concept of accident and narrow constructions of intentional conduct.

In property insurance, the issues are similar. Some cases are clear; for example, an insured who commits arson, i.e., who intentionally destroys property in which the insured has an interest, has committed an intentional act, and its consequences are outside the coverage. At the other

---

8 *See C.M. Life Ins. Co. v. Ortega*, 562 So.2d 702 (Fla. App. 1990).

9 *See*, e.g., *Moore v. Life Ins. Co. of N. Am.*, 708 F.Supp.2d 597 (N.D. W.Va. 2010). For more discussion, *see* Douglas R. Richmond, *Drunk in the Serbonian Bog: Intoxicated Drivers' Deaths as Insurance Accidents*, 32 SEATTLE U. L. REV. 83 (2008).

10 *Compare Weil v. Federal Kemper Life Assur. Co.*, 866 P.2d 774 (Cal. en banc 1994) (no coverage) *with Jessen v. Cigna Group Ins. & Life Ins. Co.*, 812 F.Supp.2d 805 (E.D. Mich. 2011) (coverage).

extreme, an insured under a homeowner's policy who negligently fails to tend to a candle, which causes a fire to start that destroys the home, has suffered an accidental loss. The in-between cases are more difficult. For example, should an insured who stores gasoline in barrels in his garage during a fuel shortage have coverage when the gasoline ignites and destroys the property? Is this mere negligence, or is it a kind of reckless behavior—by analogy to driving while intoxicated with death resulting—that should eliminate coverage under the logic that storing the gasoline is an intentional act which carries such a high risk of loss that the insured should expect the loss, and thereby be denied coverage? These cases have proved difficult enough that most insurers address such situations with an *increase of hazard clause*, which excludes coverage for losses resulting from a new use of the property or a physical change in the condition of the property, within the knowledge and control of the insured, which increases the insurer's risk.

Another vexing problem involving property insurance and intentional loss is whether the rights of an innocent co-insured are affected by the intentional acts of another co-insured. This question can arise in any situation where jointly owned property is insured under a policy purchased jointly to cover the joint interest, but the recurring fact pattern involves a marital or cohabitation relationship where one partner, in a deliberate effort to inflict abuse on the other, intentionally destroys or damages the jointly owned property. Insurers initially denied coverage in these cases under the logic that providing coverage would unjustly reward the wrongdoer, but this answer also punishes an innocent co-insured—who in the archetypal case is already the victim of other intimate partner abuse. Either by court decision or legislative action, the modern rule elevates the social imperative of protecting victims of intimate partner violence and upholds coverage in these situations, even though the loss is caused intentionally.[11]

9.2.2 Third-party insurance: liability insurance

The justification for excluding coverage when an insured intentionally causes injury or damage to a third party's interest is obvious. Premiums

---

11 For more discussion, see Hazel Glenn Beh, *Tort Liability for Intentional Acts of Family Members: Will Your Insurer Stand By You?*, 68 TENN. L. REV. 1 (2000).

are based on the probabilities of accidental losses; if the insured controls the risk, which is the case with intentional acts, the insurer's ability to calculate appropriate premiums is frustrated. Moreover, policyholders who do not engage in intentional or reckless conduct that hurts others do not want to pay higher premiums to subsidize those who do. In addition, most agree that public policy is frustrated if an insurance law rule allows willful wrongdoers to escape the financial consequences of their misbehaviors. That being said, as with first-party insurance, these generalizations do not provide complete answers for all situations.

The initial question is whether the perspective of the insured or the third-party victim should be used to determine whether a loss is accidental.[12] Recall that in life insurance, the insured's intentional self-destruction does not eliminate the payment of benefits to the third-party beneficiary. Similarly, in liability insurance, the victim of the policyholder's conduct seeks compensation under the contract between policyholder and insurer; if compensation is the goal, perhaps the policyholder's state of mind should not matter. (Indeed, with respect to compulsory automobile liability insurance in the US, many state statutes provide that the liability insurer cannot refuse coverage when the insured intentionally uses an automobile to injure another.) One distinction is that the life insurance beneficiary is designated by the policyholder (which creates an expectation in the third party, although the law imposes no requirement that the beneficiary know of the designation as a prerequisite to receiving proceeds), whereas third-party victims of a policyholder's wrongful conduct are unknown at the time the liability policy is issued and therefore have no specific expectations about coverage. Moreover, nothing prevents individuals, who are presumed to be aware of the law's rule that liability insurance does not cover liability for wrongful acts intentionally inflicted on others, from purchasing first-party insurance that indemnifies against losses suffered because of the non-covered behaviors of others. Thus, the general rule is that whether an event is intentional or accidental for purposes of liability coverage is viewed from the perspective of the policyholder, not the third-party victim.

---

12 Some policies use the word "accident" as the label for the event that triggers coverage. Many forms, especially commercial forms, use the word "occurrence" to describe the triggering event, but "occurrence" is then typically defined as an "accident." *See* JERRY & RICHMOND, pp. 431–438.

At this juncture, two more important questions present themselves. First, is it necessary that the insured has subjective intent to injure or damage another, or is it sufficient that a reasonable, objective person in the shoes of the insured intends the act and expects injury or damage to occur as a result? Second, is it sufficient that the act be intentional for the event to be deemed outside the coverage, or is necessary that the insured intends the result as well?

The first question acknowledges that a difference exists between acting with an intent or desire to harm and acting with the anticipation that harm will result. If an anticipation standard is used, the scope of coverage will be narrowed, perhaps substantially. For example, an automobile driver who greatly exceeds the speed limit may neither intend nor desire to hurt anyone, nor may the driver subjectively expect this will happen. But if a reasonable person, objectively speaking, should anticipate that speeding to this excess is likely to lead to an accident injurious to a third party, labeling this conduct "intentional" for purposes of the liability policy's coverage would eliminate compensation for any victims of such conduct, compromising the public policy favoring compensation for injured third parties. Moreover, what constitutes "anticipation of a result" is subject to interpretation. As a general matter, anticipating or expecting something presumes that the injury or damage has a high probability of occurring as a consequence of the insured's act or omission, but whether this translates as something needing to be "practically certain," "substantially certain," "substantially probable," or "reasonably foreseeable" to be intended is reasonably debatable. This is further complicated by the language in many liability policies that a loss is excluded if it is "intended or expected" from the insured's viewpoint.

The second question—whether the act or the result (or both) must be intentional—has additional implications for the scope of coverage. The most common answer to this question is that for a loss to be excluded, the insured must intend both to act and to cause some kind of harm, and it is not essential that the harm which results is the same as the harm that was intended. Thus, under this rule, if Alpha throws a punch at Beta intending to break Beta's nose but misses and hits Gamma and breaks Gamma's nose instead, the fact that the resulting harm is different from what Alpha intended does not make the loss unintentional. A court more concerned about compensating Gamma for Gamma's loss might apply a different test—that the loss is outside coverage only if the harm which results is the same as what the policyholder intended. Thus, under this alternative test, Gamma would have coverage for the resulting injury—whereas if Alpha's aim had been better and Beta's nose were broken, Beta would not be entitled to obtain compensation from Alpha's liability policy.

The majority rule places more emphasis on ensuring that wrongdoers are personally responsible for their conduct than on compensating those injured by their conduct. This point of view stresses that insurance rules should not frustrate the deterrence rationale of tort rules; that is, if wrongdoers know insurance will pay for the consequences of their wrongs, wrongful conduct will not be deterred by the underlying tort rule. Those advocating a narrower intentional act exclusion acknowledge that in the absence of coverage victims still possess a claim against the wrongdoer, but most wrongdoers lack personal assets sufficient to pay their liabilities, which means that as a practical matter, victims are uncompensated in the absence of effective liability insurance.

In short, the meaning of "accident" and the understanding of what constitutes an "intentional act" have profound implications for the scope of liability insurance coverage. They also are relevant to important public policy questions, including the balance between compensating victims of wrongs and enforcing individual responsibility.[13]

9.3 Causation

In ordinary usage, the term causation refers to the relationship between an event or act (or failure to act) and the result. The term carries this same meaning in legal usage, with the important caveat that in many situations causation is a prerequisite to responsibility or liability. For example, a negligent actor is not liable in tort for an injury unless the negligence caused the injury, a contract breacher is not liable for losses of the promisee not caused by the breach, and so on.

Legal usage also distinguishes between two different kinds of causation. When one inquires into the *cause in fact*, the question is whether an act or event was the actual cause of the result; the answer will be "yes"

---

13 For more discussion, *see* Jerry & Richmond, pp. 393–405, 431–438.

if the result would not have occurred without the act or event. When one inquires into the *proximate cause* or the *legal cause*, the question is whether the act or event has legal significance, and this requires that the cause be primary or dominant in a chain of causation (i.e., when events unfold in a linear fashion, as when A causes B, and then B causes C, and so on) or in a net of causation (i.e., when independent events operate concurrently to produce a loss, as when A and B operate independently and concurrently to produce C). Thus, to be a proximate or legal cause, it is sometimes said that the cause in question cannot be too remote from the result but need not be the last event that occurs before the result. Under another formulation, it is said that to be a proximate or legal cause, the result must be a reasonably foreseeable consequence of the act or event and must not be the result of an abnormal sequence that was unforeseeable to the actor.

In sum, cause-in-fact analysis simply inquires into whether the act, occurrence, or event actually produced the result, whereas proximate or legal causation analysis involves a more subjective assessment of whether liability ought to be imposed in the circumstances. One prominent treatise explains it this way—that proximate cause imposes subjective limits on the scope of legal liability based on "our more or less inadequately expressed ideas of what justice demands, or of what is administratively possible and convenient."[14]

Insurance law routinely deals with questions of causation because the language of cause and effect is used to define the scope of the insurer's obligation to the policyholder. In *specified-risk policies*, the insuring agreement states that the insurer will pay for losses caused by covered perils specifically listed and defined in the policy. When the policyholder suffers a loss and submits a claim for proceeds, the policy language requires a cause-in-fact inquiry where the question is whether the loss resulted from a peril listed in the policy, and the evidentiary burden is placed on the policyholder to establish the causal connection. In *all-risk policies*, the insuring agreement states that the insurer will pay for all losses of a described kind, and the policyholder's evidentiary burden is simply to establish that a loss happened. Both kinds of policies have exclusions which state that coverage does not exist if the loss is caused by

---

14 W. Keeton et al., Prosser and Keeton on the Law of Torts, p. 264 (5th ed. 1984).

certain perils, and a cause-in-fact inquiry is required where the evidentiary burden is placed on the insurer to establish the causal connection between an exclusion and the loss. In short, causation is fundamental to coverage; in both coverage grants and exclusions, it is common for the scope of coverage to be defined in terms of causation.

Like other fields of law, insurance law routinely confronts the situation where an event results from a combination of causes occurring sequentially or concurrently (or both). When a policyholder makes a claim under a policy for a loss that results from a mix of covered and excluded causes,[15] a rule is needed to determine whether the loss is covered. Essentially three options[16] exist for the rule: (1) if a covered cause contributes in any respect to the loss, the entire loss is covered; (2) if an excluded cause contributes in any respect to the loss, the entire loss is not covered; (3) when covered and excluded causes combine to produce a loss, coverage will turn on whether the dominant cause is within or outside the coverage. The first two options are easier to apply than the third, in that the presence of a cause pointing for or against coverage anywhere in the sequence, regardless of its significance in the combination, determines the result. The first option favors the policyholder, and the second favors the insurer. The third option requires a fact-based assessment of the combination of causes to determine which was the most important or significant in the array. This option is a better fit with what objectively reasonable persons in the position of the contracting parties would say "caused" a loss if they were asked to explain what happened. Many courts have embraced the

---

15 A third kind of cause exists in theory—causes that are neither covered nor excluded, in the sense that the policy language does not address them one way or another. Because all-risk policies cover losses without regard to cause unless the cause is specifically excluded, a cause that is not mentioned in an all-risk policy is, by default, covered. In specified-risk policies, a cause of loss that is not covered will not produce coverage in the first instance, and thus the question of concurrent causation cannot arise.

16 Other possibilities exist. For example, one could apply a rule that treats the first (or the last) cause in a temporal sequence as the dispositive cause. Similarly, one could apply a rule that treats the cause most geographically or spatially proximate to the location of the loss as the dispositive cause. These alternatives are usually rejected as arbitrary constructs that only coincidentally match up with "the most important" cause in a sequence or other combination. This critique is persuasive, but it is also fair to wonder why a rule that turns on the mere presence of an excluded cause in a sequence or other combination, regardless of its significance to the loss, is any less arbitrary.

logic of the third option, sometimes labeling this rule as the *efficient cause* or *efficient proximate cause doctrine.*

The choice of rule is ultimately a decision about the scope of coverage. Of the three options, the first is the most generous, pro-policyholder view of coverage, and the second is the narrowest articulation of coverage. The third option, the efficient cause rule, sits between the two. To illustrate how it works, imagine a property insurance policy that covers the loss of a house due to fire, but excludes coverage for loss due to earthquake. An earthquake causes shifts in the earth beneath a house, and this causes a break in a natural gas line; natural gas escapes, and open wires severed due to the earthquake ignite the gas, and the ensuing fire destroys the house. Was the loss caused by earthquake or fire? Under option two, the policyholder has no chance of prevailing under any understanding of the facts because earthquake is a contributing factor to the loss; the coverage is narrow. Under the efficient cause rule, the policyholder can make a plausible argument that fire, a covered cause, destroyed the house, whereas the earthquake alone, although it set the sequence in motion, would not have destroyed the house. The insurer will argue, of course, that the earthquake was the dominant cause in the sequence, without which no loss would have occurred. The essence of the insurer's argument would be that if someone asked the insured how their home was destroyed, the answer would be "it was one of the homes destroyed in the Great Earthquake of '26," not "we lost it in a fire."

Insurance companies, of course, control the language of the policies they sell, and they dislike legal rules that have flexibility regarding matters of coverage. Thus, many insurers have responded with policy language that essentially establishes the second option as the governing rule as a matter of contractual agreement. This language is known as the *anti-concurrent causation provision.* Formulated in varied ways, one common provision reads as follows:

> We will not pay for loss or damage caused directly or indirectly by any of the following: [list of exclusions follows.] *Such loss or damage is excluded regardless of any other cause or event that contributes concurrently or in any sequence to the loss.* [emphasis added][17]

---

17 Insurance Services Office, Inc., Causes of Loss-Special Form, CP 10 30 10 12 (2011).

The intent of this language is to bind the policyholder to the narrow conception of coverage (the second option) as a matter of contract law. Most courts in the US have enforced this language as the insurers intend it, but a few courts have reasoned that the efficient cause doctrine is an immutable rule that cannot be modified by the language of the policy.[18] Courts that have so held are essentially declaring that in matters of causation, public policy requires that a broader view of coverage prevail.[19]

---

18 *See*, e.g., *Safe Ins. Co. of Am. v. Hirschmann*, 773 P.2d 413 (Wash. 1989); *Murray v. State Farm Fire & Cas. Co.*, 509 S.E.2d 1 (W. Va. 1998).

19 For more discussion of causation in insurance, *see* Jerry & Richmond, pp. 466–472.

10 Liability insurance: indemnity, defense, and settlement obligations

As discussed in Chapter 4, first-party insurance provides coverage for damage to the policyholder's interests in life or property. In some circumstances, that damage may have been caused by a third party. If that is the situation, and if the third party is legally responsible for the damage under the law of tort or a statute, the victim's successful assertion of that claim, regardless of whether the victim has first-party insurance covering the damage, will shift the loss from the victim to the third party. Liability insurance is a kind of insurance that covers this third party's risk of being sued for an alleged liability to someone else and, if the assertion of that claim is successful, being required to indemnify the victim for the loss. Thus, when a victim suffers a loss, it may turn out that the victim will be able to shift that loss to the wrongdoer's liability insurer—and if a first-party insurer paid the victim's loss, that first-party insurer may be able to shift the loss to the wrongdoer's liability insurer as well by asserting a subrogation right.

Thus, liability insurance is a contract between a policyholder and insurer for the risk of prospective liabilities. Proceeds are paid to third parties, i.e., victims of the insured's wrongful conduct, which is why liability insurance is often referred to as third-party insurance. The laws that create legal liabilities and the policies that insure them have a deep and complex symbiotic relationship, and this important interconnection raises a variety of legal questions that do not arise in other lines of insurance.[1]

---

1 In the US since 1923, the American Legal Institute (ALI) has prepared *Restatements of the Law* in particular subject matter areas for the purpose of distilling the law from cases and statutes, indicating trends in the common law, and occasionally recommending what a rule of law should be. In 2018,

10.1 The relationship between tort liability and liability insurance

Tort law is the law of civil liability for wrongs (other than breach of contract) that cause a claimant to suffer loss or harm. Without tort law (and analogous statutory rights, which for the purposes of this discussion are grouped within the term "tort law"), there is no need for liability insurance. Without liability insurance, tort victims have less (and often no) interest in pursuing claims against tortfeasors because most tortfeasors lack the financial resources to pay the damages awarded. This interconnected relationship of liability insurance and tort law is evident in tort law's early history. When legislatures and courts in the mid-nineteenth century relaxed the barriers to employees holding employers liable for workplace injuries, insurers almost as quickly brought employers liability insurance to the market.[2] As liabilities expanded, insurers recognized the growing market for liability insurance products, and by the early twentieth century, the typical liability policy sold in the US provided broad protection "against the legal liability of the Assured arising from bodily injuries resulting from negligence."[3] These developments paralleled the expansion of liability insurance in Europe.[4]

Liability insurance has been shaped by the growth of tort liability, but it is also true that liability insurance controls how tort law is operation-

---

the ALI approved the *Restatement of the Law, Liability Insurance*, which states basic liability insurance contract rules, principles regarding defense, settlement, and cooperation obligations, and general principles on coverage and remedies. The project sparked significant insurance industry opposition, but numerous courts have used the new *Restatement* in recent cases. As of 2022, whether the ALI will embark on a *Restatement* project for first-party insurance is not yet known. As discussed in more detail in Chapter 5, footnote 3, in 2015, a project group in Europe approved a statement of *Principles of European Insurance Contract Law (PEICL)*, which compiles and restates rules applying to private insurance, but not reinsurance.

2 *See* Sylvester C. Dunham, *Liability Insurance*, in II YALE INSURANCE LECTURES 233 (1903–04).

3 R.S. Keelob, *Liability Policy Forms*, in II THE BUSINESS OF INSURANCE: A TEXT BOOK AND REFERENCE WORK COVERING ALL LINES OF INSURANCE (Howard P. Dunham, ed.), p. 214 (1912).

4 *See* GERHARD WAGNER, TORT LAW AND LIABILITY INSURANCE (2005) (Vol. 16 of TORT AND INSURANCE LAW).

alized.[5] The presence or absence of insurance influences whether and against whom claims are brought. When liability insurance is present, insurance influences how plaintiffs' counsels manage and try the cases. Policy limits affect the amount of damages plaintiffs seek and what they ultimately recover. Claims are shaped and pleaded to fit coverage grants and to avoid exclusions. The liability insurer usually chooses the attorney who provides the defense and exercises significant control on how cases are litigated. In almost all settlement negotiations (which is how most claims are resolved), how much coverage exists, how much insurers will contribute, and which insurers will contribute and in what amounts when multiple policies apply are invariably important negotiation points.

Liability insurance also influences the rules of tort law. In recent decades, recurring cycles in which liability insurance becomes expensive or less accessible have prompted tort reform movements. In the US, these have led to reduced legal obligations for hospitals and health care professionals, businesses, municipalities, and utilities. Typically, these take the form of restrictions on remedies for tortious conduct, including dollar ceilings on compensatory damages and limitations on punitive damages.[6]

At a more theoretical level, liability insurance is the major variable affecting whether tort law can achieve its purposes.[7] If the purpose of tort law is to incentivize potential wrongdoers to implement cost-justified measures that minimize the costs of accidents (including the costs of avoiding them),[8] liability insurance will promote or hinder achieving this goal depending on whether it is efficiently priced and regulated. If the purpose of tort law is promoting corrective justice, meaning the nullification of losses and gains that occur between individuals when one person

---

5 *See* Tom Baker, *Liability Insurance as Tort Regulation: Six Ways that Liability Insurance Shapes Tort Law in Action*, 12 Conn. Ins. L. J. 1 (2005).

6 *See* Stephen D. Sugarman, *United States Tort Reform Wars* (Aug. 2002), https://www.law.berkeley.edu/files/United States_Tort_Reform_Wars_A.TORTS.pdf. For a list of state tort law reforms in the US, *see* Ronen Avraham, *Database of State Tort Law Reforms (7.1)* (Oct. 26, 2021), https://papers.ssrn.com/sol3/papers.cfm?abstract_id=902711.

7 *See* Steven Shavell, Economic Analysis of Accident Law, pp. 186–227, 235–245 (1987); Gerhard Wagner, *Tort Law and Liability Insurance*, 31 Geneva Papers on Risk and Ins. 277 (April 2006).

8 *See* Don Dewees et al., Exploring the Domain of Accident Law: Taking the Facts Seriously, p. 5 (1996).

wrongs another,[9] liability insurance arguably frustrates this purpose when wrongdoers are allowed to shift their responsibility to an insurer, thereby escaping both the burden of compensation and the deterrence effect of remedies. Yet if one views the purchase of insurance as anticipation of the imposition of risk one's activities will impose on others, the purchase of liability insurance is arguably a form of corrective justice.[10] If the purpose of tort law is compensation, tort law cannot achieve its purposes without the existence of liability insurance.[11]

10.2 The duty to indemnify and the duty to defend

Liability risk has two main components. The first is the *indemnity risk*, which refers to the risk that someone (i.e., the wrongdoer) will become obligated to make payments, pursuant to a judgment or settlement, to a third party (i.e., the victim) because of an act or neglect for which the law imposes liability. The second is the *defense risk*, which refers to the costs, which can be substantial, of defending a claim made by a third party that an obligation to indemnify the victim's loss exists. Most liability policies cover both risks, but it is possible to buy liability insurance covering only one, i.e., *indemnity-only liability insurance* leaves the insured responsible for paying defense costs, and *defense-only liability insurance* does not cover settlement or indemnity payments. In the insuring agreement, the insurer typically promises to pay those sums that the insured becomes legally obligated to pay as damages on account of an occurrence covered by the policy, subject to the limits set forth in the declarations. The insuring agreement will also typically state that the insurer has a duty—and a right—to defend any suit seeking those damages. The promise to defend is ordinarily not subject to any cap or limit, but some policies known as *defense-within-limits policies* (or *burning-limits policies*) deduct defense cost expenditures from the indemnity limits.

---

9 *See* Catharine P. Wells, *Tort Law as Corrective Justice: A Pragmatic Justification for Jury Adjudication*, 88 MICH. L. REV. 2348, 2350, 2355 (1990).

10 For more discussion, *see* Gary T. Schwartz, *The Ethics and the Economics of Tort Liability Insurance*, 75 CORNELL L. REV. 313 (1990).

11 See DEWEES ET AL., supra n. 8, p. 7.

Both coverages are valuable to the insured. The insured has an obvious interest in preserving the value of one's assets if an obligation to indemnify someone else's loss is imposed. Also, the costs of defending against a third party's claim can be substantial, but liability insurance permits the policyholder to turn the claim over to the insurer with the expectation that the insurer will use its expertise and resources to defend the policyholder. Even when a claim is groundless or frivolous, the plaintiff has no reasonable prospect of success, and no reasonable prospect exists that the duty to indemnity will be triggered, the insurer's duty to defend still has substantial value.

Which coverage—indemnity or defense—is broader? Despite the frequent and mistaken statement that the duty to defend is broader, the scope of coverage is the same for both duties. This is because the insurer must indemnify judgments or settlements for successful claims against the insured *within coverage*, and the insurer must defend claims filed against the insured that are *within that same coverage*. The duty to defend seems broader because it is triggered more often. The insurer must defend all claims within coverage filed against the insured, but not all these claims will trigger the duty to indemnify—because some of them will be successfully defended and no liability requiring the insurer's indemnification will exist. In other words, the coverage is the same for both duties, but the coverage will be triggered less frequently for the indemnification duty.

The policy language under which insurers assume a *duty* to defend also gives insurers a *right* to defend.[12] The rationale for this language is that an insurer which defends also wants to control the defense, so that it can choose proven and competent counsel to represent the insured and exercise some controls over litigation expenses and strategies. With control, the insurer can participate in decisions and use its expertise to identify inflated and meritless claims, assess the value of claims for settlement purposes, and prevent collusion between the insured and the victim. Collusion is rare, but some insureds, remorseful about a victim's loss and perhaps their own conduct (especially in circumstances where the insured knew the victim before the occurrence), affirmatively desire that the insurer provide compensation to the victim, even in situations where liability cannot be proved. In addition, insureds and victims have occa-

---

12 *See* Douglas R. Richmond, *Liability Insurers' Right to Defend their Insureds*, 35 CREIGHTON L. REV. 115 (2001).

sionally collaborated in schemes to defraud insurers. Having the ability to control the insured's defense using counsel selected by the insurer reduces the likelihood that the insured will cooperate with the victim to the detriment of the insurer.

If the policy language did not give insurers the right to defend, insureds could choose their own counsel and defend themselves—at the insurer's expense. Although many insureds would prefer to hand off the defense to the insurer and relinquish control if they had the option, in some circumstances, an insured might prefer to take a case to trial when the insurer would be more inclined to settle. For example, an insured with a reputation interest at stake, such as a physician whose competence is questioned in a malpractice suit, or a restaurant that is sued by customers for food poisoning, might want a full-throated, unconstrained defense by an attorney of their choosing in aggressive pursuit of a zero verdict and vindication. But giving this control to the insured is not the deal that insurers are willing to make—unless the policyholder is willing to pay a higher premium to retain this control. Except for cases involving the most sophisticated insureds, because the insurer is a repeat player in defending covered claims and has greater capacity to manage litigation, the insurer can provide a higher-quality defense at a lower cost than if the insured selected and retained its own counsel.

10.3 Determining when a duty to defend exists

The starting point for determining whether a duty to defend exists is examining the allegations of the complaint filed against the insured. If the complaint states facts which, if proved, would make the insured liable to pay for a loss within coverage, the insurer's duty to defend is triggered. Beyond this simple starting point, different approaches exist for determining whether a duty exists.

Some jurisdictions follow the *eight-corners rule*, which reasons that if the allegations within the complaint (i.e., within the "four corners" of the written complaint) align with the policy's coverage (i.e., within the "four corners" of the written policy), the insurer owes the duty to defend. Allegations outside these eight corners do not trigger the duty. The upshot of the eight-corners rule is that if a covered claim can be imagined from the circumstances but is not alleged, the insurer need not defend. However, if the complaint is amended to allege facts that raise covered claims, the duty to defend is triggered. The key point is that under the eight-corners rule, there must be an actual pleading alleging a covered claim, not mere awareness of or speculation about the existence of covered claims.

The eight-corners rule's virtues are simplicity and predictability. The rule also saves insurers the expenses of investigation whenever a complaint is filed to ensure that no potential, unalleged claim arising out of the facts exists; these reduced costs presumably translate into lower premiums and greater availability of coverage. The rule's weakness is that whether the insured receives a defense is controlled by what the plaintiff alleges. Plaintiffs usually try to allege claims within coverage so that they can access a source of compensation, but under the eight-corners rule, sloppy pleading can prevent an insured from receiving an insurer-provided defense (for which the insured paid a premium), even if the insurer is aware of facts which, if pleaded, would trigger the duty.

Some courts have expanded the eight-corners rule to require a defense when allegations in the complaint, although not specifically alleging facts within coverage, suggest the potential for coverage. Under this rule, which is usually labeled the *potentiality rule*, a complaint alleging that the insured "intentionally rammed his car into plaintiff" would not allege coverage because intentional acts are within an exclusion to coverage. But if the complaint alleged that the insured's car "struck the plaintiff," this allegation, on its face, has the potential for coverage because the striking could be negligent and within coverage. Under this version of the rule, the insurer can limit its analysis to what is in the complaint and need not make any investigation into the circumstances raised by the complaint.

Other courts have taken the potentiality rule a step farther to impose a duty on the insurer to consider facts extrinsic to the complaint of which it is, or reasonably should be, aware when evaluating its duty to defend. These may be facts brought to the insurer's attention or facts that the insurer could reasonably discover when investigating whether it has a duty to defend. If these additional facts give rise to the insured's potential liability, the insurer has a duty to defend. This expanded version of the potentiality rule is commonly referred to as the *extrinsic evidence rule*. Under this rule, the significance of evidence outside the complaint usually operates only in one direction, i.e., to expand the obligation to defend. In other words, the insurer cannot use extrinsic evidence to show that allegations in the complaint are incorrect or untrue and thereby defeat the duty to defend. This is because the insurer has a duty to defend even groundless and frivolous claims within coverage, and extrinsic evidence showing that the pleaded facts are incorrect does not eliminate the duty.

If the extrinsic evidence relates to coverage, however, and if the undisputed evidence unequivocally shows that the claims are outside coverage, most courts allow the insurer to withdraw from the defense. Under the logic of this qualification, courts do not require an insurer to defend a stranger if the complaint falsely alleges that the defendant was the insurer's policyholder, or to defend the insured if all the relevant events happened at times outside the period when the policy was in effect. In other words, a situation where the undisputed extrinsic facts establish no liability for a covered claim is treated differently from a situation where the undisputed extrinsic facts show that no coverage could possibly exist.

When drafting a complaint, a plaintiff's counsel will ordinarily allege every possible legal theory that might support recovery under the facts as they are known at the time of filing. Also, because plaintiffs are more likely to obtain compensation if liability insurance is available, counsel are incentivized to shape a complaint to allege at least one claim within coverage. Consequently, the situation where a complaint alleges both covered and non-covered claims is common. Because the insurer has a contractual duty to defend covered claims, it would make little sense if the simultaneous pleading of a non-covered claim discharged the insurer's duty, and that is not the rule. Thus, when covered and non-covered claims arise out of the same set of facts, the insurer must also assume responsibility to defend the non-covered claim. If, however, the allegations made in one complaint can be separated (as when one set of allegations arises out of one set of facts and another set arises out of an independent set of facts), then it is fair for the insurer to confine its defense to the covered claims and to leave to the insured the defense of the claims outside coverage.

The presence of covered and non-covered claims in the same complaint can, however, create tension between the insurer and insured. This tension can arise in other ways as well. When this happens, it has implications for how the duty to defend is operationalized, and this is discussed in the next subsection.[13]

10.4 Potential tension between the insurer's and insured's interests

In most situations where a victim sues the insured-tortfeasor, the claim is within coverage, the amount sought as damages is equal to or less than the limits of the policy, and no extraneous factors exist that give the insured a special reason to care about how the claim is defended. In these full-coverage situations, the insurer bears all the risk, and the insured is ordinarily pleased to turn the defense over to the insurer and put the case out of mind, while remaining available to cooperate with the insurer when requested. Sometimes, however, the insured bears some of the risk, and this creates the potential for the insurer's and insured's interests to diverge. This can happen when the plaintiff seeks damages exceeding the policy limits, when one or more claims are or may be outside the coverage, or when the insured is worried about a risk not covered by the policy (such as damage to reputation or potential criminal liability). Any of these situations may cause the insured to desire that the case be defended in a particular way or perhaps settled within policy limits, while the insurer simultaneously believes the case would be better defended in some other manner.

Complexity is added by the fact that the insurer and insured are not the only entities interacting in the defense of the case; the attorney selected by the insurer to represent the insured is also a player in what is essentially a tripartite relationship. The attorney has obligations to the insurer by virtue of the retainer agreement between attorney and insurer. The attorney also assumes obligations to the insured by virtue of a retainer agreement the attorney will form with the insured. This retainer agreement will be written in terms that implement the insurer's obligations to the insured under the insurance contract. Further, the attorney's

13 For more discussion, *see* Douglas R. Richmond, *Using Extrinsic Evidence to Excuse a Liability Insurer's Duty to Defend*, 74 SMU L. REV. 119 (2021); Ellen S. Pryor, *The Tort Liability Regime and the Duty to Defend*, 58 MD. L. REV. 1 (1999); JERRY & RICHMOND, pp. 691–732.

obligations to both insurer and insured, who are clients (at least until the tension ripens into a conflict), are governed by the rules of professional conduct—essentially, the law governing lawyering, which regulates attorneys in their professional relationships with their clients, other parties, and the court. These rules allow co-client representation in the absence of a serious, nonwaivable conflict of interests between or among co-clients. Full-coverage defenses present no conflict (absent very unusual circumstances), but when the insured also bears risk, the attorney must assess whether a potential or actual conflict between insurer and insured prohibits joint representation.

If a conflict rises to that level, the insured must be represented by independent counsel, meaning an attorney who owes undivided loyalty and allegiance to the insured and is outside the control of the insurer. In most jurisdictions when this happens, the insured is allowed to select their own attorney, with reasonable fees and costs to be paid by the insurer. The logic of this rule is that a lawyer selected by the insurer will inevitably favor the interests of the insurer (either consciously or subconsciously), most likely in the hope of securing repeat business, and only if the insured selects one's own attorney will that lawyer's undivided loyalty to the insured be guaranteed. In a minority of jurisdictions, the insurer selects the attorney (and pays the fees) but instructs the attorney that the insured is the attorney's sole client. This viewpoint reasons that ethics rules and the threat of malpractice liability provide sufficient incentive for counsel appointed by an insurer to faithfully serve the insureds they are hired to represent.

In many situations where the insured retains some risk, defense counsel can conduct the defense without favoring the insurer or compromising the insured's interests because the facts to be decided in the plaintiff's lawsuit do not implicate the conflict between insurer and insured. For example, if the insurer wishes to contest coverage on the ground that the insured failed to satisfy a condition or duty under the policy (e.g., timely notice, cooperation with the insurer during investigation, etc.) or misrepresented a material fact in the application, the plaintiff's claim can be defended to the point of a judgment or settlement, and what happens in that litigation will not affect the potential basis for the insurer denying coverage. In such instances, the common procedure is for the insurer to notify the insured that it will provide *a defense under reservation of rights* to later contest coverage, and then, once that written notice is given, the insurer proceeds with the defense of the plaintiff's claim. This protects the insurer's interest in controlling the defense, while it *conditionally* gives the insured the benefit of the defense.

Defending under reservation of rights is usually an efficient way to manage the tension between insurer and insured. A shared interest of insurer and insured is that the plaintiff's claim be defeated; if that happens, the insurer does not need a resolution of the underlying coverage question. If the plaintiff prevails, the insurer has reserved its right to contest coverage in a subsequent proceeding (with different counsel) and may proceed to do so. In these situations and others like them, the attorney who defended the plaintiff's action will have no contact with the evidence or fact questions on which the insurer's coverage defense would turn, and, of course, would not represent either party in any subsequent coverage dispute.

Defending under reservation has another important advantage for the insurer. If the insurer had chosen not to defend based on the coverage defense and it were later determined that the insurer's coverage defense was invalid, the insurer's failure to defend would constitute a breach of the duty to defend, which would make the insurer liable for all the consequences that flow from that breach of contract—not to mention that the insurer would have lost control of the defense, thereby assuming all the vulnerabilities associated with letting unknown counsel selected by the insured handle the litigation.

The reservation of rights approach, however, cannot deal adequately with all conflicts, including the situation presented when facts exist common to both the plaintiff's allegations and the insurer's position that no coverage exists. For example, if the plaintiff's claims against the insured include both covered and non-covered claims, the insured (and the insurer) will prefer that the plaintiff fail on all claims, but if the plaintiff prevails, the insured will prefer that the basis for the judgment be a covered claim, while the insurer will prefer that the basis for the judgment be a non-covered claim. When fact issues that determine the insured's liability to plaintiff are intermingled with resolving the coverage question, an attorney cannot serve both the insurer's and insured's interests fully. If the attorney appointed by the insurer attempts to represent both insurer and insured, a risk exists that the defense will be handled in a manner that advantages the insurer's coverage defenses. In the past, the insurance industry has argued that the professional judgment of lawyers appointed by insurers to defend the insured in these situations is sufficient to protect insureds, but most courts require an independent defense to safeguard the insured's interests and to avoid the appearance of partiality—and to avoid the possibility of a subsequent allegation by the insured that defense counsel appointed by the insurer sabotaged the insured's interests. Thus, this kind of situation is one where an insured needs to be represented by independent counsel.[14]

10.5 Settlement obligations

Liability insurance policies typically reserve to the insurer a right to settle, or not settle, claims against the insured as the insurer sees fit. Most policies also contain language that prohibits the insured from settling any claims or injecting itself into settlement negotiations without the insurer's consent. For full-coverage defenses where the insured bears no risk, the insurer's reserved settlement privilege presents no concerns, and it fits nicely with the insurer's right to control the defense. When, however, the possibility of a judgment exceeding the policy limits exists, the insured also bears risk, and the insurer's decisions about settlement have a direct impact on the policyholder. If the insurer declines an offer to settle a case within the policy limits under the reasoning that the defense will prevail at trial, but this turns out to be incorrect and a judgment exceeding the policy limits is entered against the insured, the insured must pay the amount of this excess judgment. Because defending the insured requires the insurer (and counsel it appoints) to act reasonably to protect the insured's interests, the duty to defend necessarily includes an obligation to respond reasonably to settlement offers. But "responding reasonably" does not require accepting all settlement offers, as some offers will be unreasonable. Thus, there is a need for a standard (because policies do not

---

14 For more discussion about tensions among insurer, defense counsel, and insured, *see* JERRY & RICHMOND, pp. 750–787; Tom Baker, *Liability Insurance Conflicts and Defense Lawyers: From Triangles to Tetrahedrons*, 4 CONN. INS. L. J. 101 (1997); Charles M. Silver & Kent Syverud, *The Professional Responsibilities of Insurance Defense Lawyers*, 45 DUKE L.J. 255 (1995).

contain one) that explains how insurers should respond when settlement offers are received.

The need for a standard is ultimately derived from the tension that exists between insurer and insured interests when a judgment in excess of the policy limits is possible. If the plaintiff makes an offer to settle at or near the policy limits, the insured has a strong interest in the offer being accepted to eliminate its risk of an excess judgment. Yet if the insurer believes a judgment near or above the policy limits is likely, the insurer has nothing to lose by litigating the case (other than defense costs) and attempting to win the case outright or obtain a low-dollar judgment. In addition, some settlement offers *should* be rejected because they are unreasonable. The optimal rule should neutralize the insurer's incentive to gamble with the insured's money by rejecting reasonable settlement offers, while preserving the insurer's discretion to reject unreasonable offers.

As explained earlier, insurance policies by their terms do not impose a "duty to settle" on insurers. Rather, insurers reserve the privilege to settle cases when they defend, which effectively means that the insurer's duty is *to make reasonable settlement decisions* on the insured's behalf. A reasonable settlement decision is one that the insurer would make if it alone were financially responsible for the full amount of the potential judgment. Another way to describe a reasonable settlement decision is that whenever an excess judgment creating exposure for the insured is possible, the insurer must respond to a settlement offer in the same manner as a reasonable insurer would respond if no policy limits existed. Under this standard, it may turn out that the insurer declines a settlement offer and an excess judgment results, but this mistake does not violate the insurer's settlement obligations if the insurer's decision was a reasonable one in the circumstances at the time the decision was made. This standard is often described as the *disregard the limits test.*

When the insurer's settlement obligation is understood as a duty to make reasonable settlement decisions, it follows that the insurer may be obligated to initiate a settlement offer on behalf of the insured in some circumstances where the plaintiff made no offer, to make counteroffers in appropriate situations, and to act reasonably during settlement negotiations. Just like the situation where the insurer is responding to a settlement offer, the question is what a reasonable insurer would do in the circumstances.

Some courts have articulated the settlement rule in other ways, such as requiring the insurer to act with due care or not to act negligently in response to settlement offers (which makes the duty sound like it resides in tort rather than contract), to give equal consideration to the insured's interests (which probably means giving less weight to the insured's interests than what happens under the disregard-the-limits test), to not subordinate the insured's interests to its own (which sounds like an instruction to the insurer to give at least equal consideration to the insured's interests), or to respond to settlement offers in good faith (which requires a further articulation of what good faith requires). These alternative standards all address the issue by ratcheting up the insurer's incentive to heed the insured's interests, but they lack the simplicity and clarity of a rule that measures the insurer's performance against what a reasonable insurer would do if no policy limits existed.[15]

10.6 Coverage: some recurring questions and issues

10.6.1 Occurrence versus claims-made coverage

Liability insurance is sold in two different formats. *Occurrence-based policies* tie coverage to an occurrence, which is usually defined as an accident or some other kind of fortuitous event which causes loss (often defined as *bodily injury or property damage*). In most policies, the injury or damage—not the accident—must occur during the policy period. In typical situations, injury or damage occurs at the same time an accident happens, but there are occasions when the accident is an exposure or continuous activity that does not generate or manifest an injury or damage until later. *Claims-made policies* tie the coverage to the filing of a claim against the insured which arises out of an occurrence. Thus, the claim must be filed during the policy period, even though the occurrence (and the injuries or damage resulting from the occurrence) happened before the claim was filed and before the policy was effective. One can understand

---

15 For more discussion of settlement obligations, *see* JERRY & RICHMOND, pp. 730–747; Leo P. Martinez, *The Restatement of the Law of Liability Insurance and the Duty to Settle*, 68 RUTGERS U. L. REV. 155 (2015).

occurrence-based coverage as looking to the future; if an event occurs and the harm was experienced during the policy term, the claim can be filed in any future year (subject to an applicable statute of limitations) and the policy will provide coverage. In contrast, claims-made coverage looks to the past; subject to an important caveat, it does not matter how long ago the event happened as long as the claim is filed during the term of policy's coverage. The caveat is that most claims-made policies have a *retroactive date* (or *retro date*) that requires that the occurrence also happen after a certain date; this prevents the policy from covering claims filed in the current year that happened in very remote years.

Occurrence-based policies protect the insured as long as the loss happened during a year the policy was active—regardless of how long it takes for the victim to file the claim (subject to any applicable statutes of limitation). If the policyholder decides to switch insurers or go without coverage entirely in the current year, the policyholder still has coverage for claims filed arising out of losses suffered in prior years under the occurrence-based policy that was in force in those prior years. With a claims-made policy, switching to a new insurer can cause a gap in coverage unless the insured can obtain a retro date that goes back to years prior to the new policy or can obtain an extended reporting period from the prior insurer to cover claims arising out of occurrences that happened before the expiration of the last policy. Claims-made policies are often less expensive, which some insureds prefer, because the insurer is better able to match premiums with expenditures for covered losses. But an insured who purchases them must be careful to coordinate the various policies in order to avoid gaps in coverage.[16]

10.6.2 "As damages" and "suits"

Liability policies commonly contain language stating, in so many words, that the insurer will pay "those sums that the insured becomes legally obligated to pay as damages" and that the insurer has the right and duty to defend lawsuits seeking those damages. The "as damages" term ordinarily has the effect of limiting the duty to defend to lawsuits seeking damages, which removes from coverage suits seeking injunctive or other equitable relief. Thus, if a plaintiff sues the insured for damages to property caused by the insured's negligent operation of machinery on adjacent land, the

16 For more discussion, *see* Jerry & Richmond, pp. 422–428.

liability policy (assuming other conditions are met) will cover the loss, but if the plaintiff sought to enjoin the insured from operating the machinery in order to prevent future damage, the policy will not apply. If the policy's language says the duty to indemnify and defend extends to "suits" seeking damages, most courts require that a complaint commencing a lawsuit must be filed to trigger coverage, but some courts interpret the language broadly to encompass non-judicial proceedings, such as hearings and other administrative proceedings initiated by government agencies. If the policy uses the word "claims" rather than "suits," then a demand in which damages are claimed may be treated as sufficient to trigger the duty to defend and indemnify.[17]

10.6.3 Triggers

As discussed above, occurrence-based policies require that the bodily injury or property damage occur during the policy's term, and when occurrences involve a sudden, sometimes violent force, the injury or damage typically occurs in the same instant that the force is expressed. But some events involve long, continuous exposures over an extended period, and the question arises as to when the injury or damage occurs in that type of event. This can be especially important when a policy was in effect for only a few years, or when successive policies issued by different insurers were purchased. Different courts have given different answers for what triggers the coverage. The *manifestation trigger* treats the injury or damage as occurring when it is discernible to the victim through experienced symptoms or visible damage. The *exposure trigger* treats the injury or damage as occurring whenever exposure to the injurious or damaging conditions happens, with the logic being that injury or damage is occurring during exposure, even if it is not discernible until later. *The injury-in-fact trigger* is usually later than exposure but earlier than manifestation; it refers to the time when the injury or damage is "real," as in, for example, the moment when the body's defenses are overwhelmed but a diagnosis is not yet possible. A fourth approach applies all the triggers simultaneously; this *multiple trigger* or *triple trigger* approach maximizes the available coverage.[18]

---

17 For more discussion, *see* JERRY & RICHMOND, pp. 432–434.

18 For more discussion, *see* JERRY & RICHMOND, pp. 438–444.

10.6.4 Number of occurrences

Another question often confronted in liability insurance is how to count the number of occurrences when one covered cause produces multiple losses: was there one occurrence, or did multiple occurrences happen? To illustrate, suppose an insured sells contaminated bird seed to five wholesalers, who in turn sell the seed to 25 stores, which together sell the seed to 250 customers, which results in the death of 350 pet birds. Is there one occurrence because there was one batch of contaminated seed, 350 occurrences because 350 birds died, or something in between?[19] The majority approach follows *cause analysis*, which means the number of occurrences depends on the number of causes, and not the number of injurious effects (called *effect analysis*). Thus, a series of adverse results will involve only one occurrence if there is "but one proximate, uninterrupted, and continuing cause which resulted in all the injuries and damages."[20] Because liability insurance policies have *per occurrence limits*, a finding that more than one occurrence happened has the effect of multiplying the insurer's potential liability—to the benefit of victims and insureds and to the detriment of insurers. But the tables are flipped if the policy has a per occurrence deductible; a finding of additional occurrences multiplies the application of the deductible, which reduces what the insurer is obligated to pay.

Two kinds of policy provisions reduce insurers' vulnerability to multiple-occurrence situations. First, in addition to per occurrence limits, liability policies typically also have *aggregate limits*. An aggregate limit states the maximum an insurer will pay in proceeds during a policy term, regardless of the number of occurrences. Thus, at a certain point, a finding of multiple occurrences arising out of a single cause (or, for that matter, multiple events giving rise to multiple judgments or settlements during a policy term) will exhaust the policy's coverage, leaving the

---

19 This hypothetical is based on *Maurice Pincoffs Co. v. St. Paul Fire & Marine Ins. Co.*, 447 F.2d 204 (5th Cir. 1971) (applying Texas law, holding that bird seed sales by an importer to eight different feed and grain dealers, which were sold to many buyers, constituted eight occurrences).

20 *Michigan Chem. Corp. v. Am. Home Assur. Co.*, 728 F.2d 374 (6th Cir. 1984) (concluding, where a chemical company accidentally shipped a toxic fire retardant instead of a livestock feed supplement, which led to the deaths of thousands of farm animals, that a single shipment was one occurrence despite multiple exposures).

insured responsible for liabilities in excess of the aggregate limit. Second, insurers now often include a provision to reduce the likelihood of finding multiple occurrences arising out of a single event. This language, which is commonly called the *unifying directive*, states, in so many words, that "repeated exposure to substantially the same general harmful conditions" will be treated as "arising out of one occurrence."[21]

It should be noted that the number-of-occurrences issue can arise in property insurance as well. The most famous property insurance case raising the issue was the September 11, 2001, terrorist attacks on the World Trade Center (WTC). A US federal court let stand a jury determination that the attacks on the WTC, where two airliners were flown into two towers by hijackers, were one occurrence, in that they arose out of one terrorist plot.[22] This decision saved the affected insurers billions of dollars and cost the plaintiffs just as much. In contrast, a UK High Court decision let stand an arbitration tribunal's decision that the terrorist attacks amounted to two "events" for purposes of aggregation under a catastrophe reinsurance policy.[23]

10.6.5 Punitive damages and liability for aggravated conduct

Punitive damages are sums awarded to a plaintiff over and above compensatory damages for the purposes of punishing a defendant for outrageous conduct and deterring others from engaging in similar conduct in the future. In situations where an insured is held liable for punitive damages, the question is whether this kind of liability is covered by liability insurance. If the policy excludes punitive questions from coverage, the question is answered "no" by the policy, but when the exclusion is absent, either a legislature by statutory rule or a court must address the question. Some statutes allow the coverage, whereas others prohibit it. When the issue is left to courts, most begin the analysis with a ruling that in the absence of an exclusion, policy language as a matter of contract provides coverage, but this leads to a second question: whether public

---

21 For more discussion of number of occurrences, *see* Jerry & Richmond, pp. 454–457.

22 *See SR Int'l Bus. Ins. Co. v. World Trade Ctr. Props.*, LLC, 467 F.3d 107 (2d Cir. 2006).

23 *See AIOI Nissay Dowa Ins. Co. Ltd. v. Heraldgen Ltd. & Ano* [2013], EWHC 154 (Comm.).

policy permits the insured to shift punitive damage liability to an insurer, i.e., whether the coverage is unenforceable as a matter of public policy.

When punitive damages are awarded, the conduct is often intentional; in this situation, subject to an important caveat discussed below, a policy's intentional act exclusion will lead to a no-coverage answer. Thus, the question is actually whether liability insurance can cover punitive damages awarded for gross, wanton, or reckless conduct. If punitive damages are intended to deter, allowing a wrongdoer to shift the liability to an insurer arguably frustrates the deterrence objective—but whether punitive damages serve a deterrence purpose with respect to reckless and wanton conduct (which is worse than negligence but is nevertheless unintentional) is debatable. Arguably, parties should be free to contract to transfer responsibility for any conduct that is less than intentional. Moreover, when punitive damages liability is vicariously imposed (as when, for example, an employer is held vicariously liable for the wrongdoing of an employee), the argument in favor of allowing insurability is stronger (and many statutes prohibiting coverage for punitive damages make an exception for liability vicariously imposed). The logic is that it is unfair, for example, to require an employer to bear punitive damage liability for the misconduct of an employee when the employer is not complicit in the conduct and, at worst, was simply negligent in the supervision of the employee.

Furthermore, the fact that alleged conduct is intentional does not automatically make it uninsurable. As discussed in Chapter 9, most policies specifically exclude damage or loss caused by intentional conduct. However, in liability insurance markets, insureds can purchase coverage for various kinds of intentional wrongdoing made unlawful by tort rules or statute. Examples include liability insurance for malicious prosecution, unfair competition, false imprisonment, invasion of privacy, various practices in the workplace (e.g., employment discrimination and wrongful termination), defamation, and trademark infringement. With respect to these coverages, the calculus is that the importance of compensation for victims outweighs whatever concerns exist that these kinds of coverage will encourage wrongful behavior or otherwise offend public policy. In addition, many liability policies have *final adjudication clauses*, which state that an intentional act or harm exclusion applies only if the legal action has been brought to a final adjudication. This means that when suits involving claims for intentional wrongdoing are settled, the final adjudication clause will often result in the insurer paying proceeds because there was no "final adjudication" of the insured's wrongdoing.

Even the fact that the insured's conduct may involve criminal liability does not make it uninsurable. For example, causing injury in the course of driving while intoxicated may lead to criminal liability and to punitive damage liability in a civil action. Although the authorities are divided (and a specific criminal act exclusion, if it exists, will be relevant), allowing the insurability of damages in this instance arguably serves an important victim-compensation purpose.

Even when punitive damages are deemed outside the coverage, the plaintiff alleging a wrong on which punitive damage liability is based will almost certainly also allege that the conduct was negligent. This will trigger the insurer's duty to defend, although one should anticipate that the insurer will defend under a reservation of rights to contest coverage later.[24]

10.7 Remedies for insurer's breach of defense and settlement obligations

If the insurer breaches the duty to defend, what the insured pays to obtain its own defense are damages the insurer owes. Because the working assumption is that final decisions in the adjudicative process are just, it follows that any judgment or settlement that results when the insured is represented by their chosen counsel will be the same as a judgment or settlement that would have been reached if the insurer had not breached and had provided counsel as the policy required. Thus, a judgment or settlement (including an excess judgment or a settlement in excess of policy limits) when the insurer breaches the duty to defend is not caused by the insurer's breach—unless some exceptional circumstance exists that makes it reasonable for a factfinder to conclude that the insurer's breach was a causal factor in increasing the amount of the judgment or settlement. That might be the situation where the insurer withdraws from the defense prematurely, thereby preventing the insured from mounting

---

24 For more discussion, *see* Tom Baker, *Reconsidering Insurance for Punitive Damages*, 1998 Wis. L. Rev. 101 (1998); Jerry & Richmond, pp. 457–462.

a successful defense, or where the insurer's breach proximately results in a default judgment being entered against the insured (as might be the case where the insurer knew that the insured could not afford to provide its own defense and had no alternative way to obtain representation).

If the insurer breaches its settlement obligations, it is a natural and foreseeable consequence of such a breach that a judgment exceeding the policy limits could be entered against the insured. Thus, the insurer in such a situation is liable for the full amount of the settlement, including the amount exceeding the policy limits.

If the insurer breaches the duty to indemnify by refusing to pay a judgment or settlement in circumstances where coverage is established, the insurer, under the same logic as above, is obligated to pay the amount of the plaintiff's recovery as damages.

However, as discussed in Chapter 8, insurance law frequently goes beyond contract law in calculating damages for an insurer's breach, and that same analysis holds when liability insurance contracts are involved. Thus, some courts and some legislatures by statutory rule expand the range of damages policyholders can recover when the insurer breaches the duty to defend. This can include damages for any excess judgment, attorneys' fees, damages for bad faith, and estopping the insurer to deny the existence of coverage if the right to contest coverage was reserved. Although contract law properly applied awards the insured an excess judgment when settlement obligations are breached, the other mentioned remedies are also available in some jurisdictions. The same is true with respect to breach of the duty to indemnify.[25]

---

25 For more discussion, *see* JERRY & RICHMOND, pp. 615–622, 716–729, 743–747.

11 Challenges in a changing world: why insurance matters (reprise)

When the discussion in Chapter 2 explained how insurance manages risk, it demonstrated the vital role insurance plays in enabling economic growth and protecting interests fundamental to our most important social relationships. In this chapter, we return to that theme and examine some pressing problems facing communities, governments, and our world. The discussion briefly explains how insurance is intertwined with the substance of each problem, and then explores how insurance law and regulation can play a role in finding solutions. The chapter closes with some observations about the connections among insurance, governance, order, and social values.

11.1 Difficult risks and catastrophic loss

The earth's climate has gone through warming and cooling cycles for hundreds of thousands of years, but the current global warming trend is unprecedented. The data show that human activities since the mid-1800s have caused the rate of acceleration in warming and the amount of greenhouse gases trapped in the atmosphere to reach their highest levels in 800,000 years.[1] Almost all scientists agree that as a direct result of these

1 For detailed discussion, *see* P.A. Arias et al., *Technical Summary*, in CLIMATE CHANGE 2021: THE PHYSICAL SCIENCE BASIS. CONTRIBUTION OF WORKING GROUP I TO THE SIXTH ASSESSMENT REPORT OF THE INTERGOVERNMENTAL PANEL ON CLIMATE CHANGE (V. Masson-Delmotte et al., eds.), pp. 33–144, https://www.ipcc.ch/report/ar6/wg1/downloads/report/IPCC_AR6_WGI_TS.pdf.

changes, “extremes” are increasing throughout the world—extreme rainfall, massive flooding, stronger hurricanes, intense heat waves, prolonged drought, more wildfires, etc. Recent decades have witnessed the costliest natural disaster events in the history of the planet.[2]

The extreme losses associated with natural disasters are difficult for private market insurance mechanisms to manage. First, natural disaster risks resist diversification, which is essential for the law of large numbers to work effectively to distribute risk. When a risk pool consists of highly correlated risks (i.e., when a very high percentage of a risk pool is likely to suffer loss when a covered peril happens), it is impossible to distribute the risk across the pool, which means the insurance mechanism fails. Second, natural disaster risks are ambiguous both in terms of their frequency and their consequences. When measuring risk is prone to inaccuracy because of unpredictable frequency and consequences, insurers either avoid the market or charge very high premiums to cover their uncertainty risk, which in turn hurts accessibility to the product and may lead to market failure. When insurance for a home or business is unavailable or unaffordable, an uninsured catastrophic loss can have adverse, multi-generational impacts for individuals and can bankrupt a business—with all the collateral damage those outcomes can produce.

Not all difficult risks are tied to climate change and weather, however. The COVID-19 pandemic reminded us that a microscopic virus has the potential to wreak catastrophic damage—in this case, the largest loss of life and destruction of economic activity from a single cause since World War II. Human agency can also produce catastrophic loss. Terrorism has the potential to cause catastrophic loss (especially if accomplished through chemical, biological, or radiological weaponry). Nuclear power plants provide essential energy resources, but they also carry very high risk, as demonstrated by the accident at the Chernobyl plant in Ukraine in 1986 and the tsunami-caused meltdown at the Fukushima plant in Japan in 2011. As discussed in Chapter 9, war has always had the potential to cause catastrophic loss, which is why insurance policies have contained exclusions for losses caused by war and other war-like conditions for decades. Humans also increase the losses suffered in natural disasters when we choose to live, as we are in increasing numbers, in vulnerable

2 *See* Ins. Inf. Inst., *Facts + Statistics: Global Catastrophes* (2022), https://www.iii.org/fact-statistic/facts-statistics-global-catastrophes.

coastal areas, flood zones, and locales with high wildfire risk, and when we decline to invest in loss mitigation practices before catastrophes occur.

Progress has been made in recent years in finding strategies to spread difficult risks, including reinsurance in global markets, securitization and catastrophe bonds, and more advanced predictive and analytic tools. Much exposure, however, is uninsured. Where the social costs of lack of access to insurance are too great, government sometimes intercedes by offering itself as the insurer of last resort. Government has the means to use its budget to spread risk throughout a very large pool (all taxpayers), thereby accomplishing risk transfer and distribution that private markets cannot provide. Government risk management tools include providing backstops to private industry losses (i.e., setting limits beyond which the government becomes the insurer), undertaking government underwriting of products sold through private companies, and providing insurance directly through a governmentally created and managed program.

The response to difficult risks must necessarily be multi-faceted. Resilience-enhancing measures to prevent loss, mitigation measures to lessen the impact of future disasters, improved response capabilities to reduce loss as events unfold, and post-loss disaster relief are all parts of a strategy for dealing with difficult risks. Insurance is obviously an important mechanism for post-loss recovery, but how it is offered and priced influences how individuals and firms plan for such events. Given that the forces that threaten catastrophic losses are escalating in strength and manifesting themselves more frequently, insurance will be a crucial part of the risk management discussion for the foreseeable future.

11.2 Technology and cyber-risk

The invention of computer technology and the information explosion accompanying it—the "digital age"—is a transformative period in human history. The universal reliance by businesses of all kinds and sizes on networks and telecommunications, hardware, software, databases, data storage facilities, and the human resources to manage the system has brought new risks. Businesses are vulnerable to cyberattacks, ransomware attacks, intellectual property theft, theft of customers' commercial and personal data, and the expenses of managing these breaches. Some of these risks involve liabilities to third parties; others involve the expenses of repairing or replacing damaged systems and data, plus the loss of income while business is interrupted. Merely managing a data breach can be expensive; fulfilling notice requirements for those affected can be costly, and regulatory fines are sometimes imposed. These attacks have increased in frequency and now cost businesses billions of dollars every year.

Cyber-insurance is currently available as both first-party and third-party coverage, but the product is only about twenty years old. The first cyber-policies were third-party policies, i.e., liability insurance, and these reimburse insureds for losses suffered by their clients and customers because of data breaches, malware and computer virus infections, and cyberattacks resulting from the fault of the insured. First-party policies reimburse insureds for their costs arising out of hacks, malware, and viruses, and attacks that affect the insured's operations. Depending on how the policy is written, it can cover data recovery costs, credit-monitoring and data breach expenses, ransom payments and the costs of negotiators to respond to ransom payment demands, and other kinds of losses. Cyber-insurance can be purchased as a stand-alone policy or as a coverage within a standard property-casualty form. Most standard forms for property and liability coverage have been revised to either cover or exclude property damage or liability arising out of cyber incidents; where excluded, the coverage can usually be brought back into the policy by endorsement.[3]

Because digital assets have become much more important, cyber-insurance has become an extremely important product, but the market for it is chaotic for several reasons. First, the risk is difficult to measure. Because the risk is new, loss histories are short, which confounds insurers' effort to price the risk. Also, past experience, to the extent it exists, is a weak predictor of future cyber events because technology, including the methods of attacking computer systems and networks, is changing so rapidly. Second, steep increases in the costs of cyberattacks have caused large increases in premiums, the tightening of policy terms, and reduced availability of coverage. Third, the risk has elements of high correlation, which, as discussed earlier in this chapter, distorts the market and can

---

3 *See* Symposium, *Insuring Against Cyber Risk: The Evolution of an Industry*, 122 PENN ST. L. REV. 607 (2018).

lead to market failure. Global interconnections and widespread reliance on computers to run critical infrastructure, including power grids, financial systems, and transportation (even modern automobiles), create the possibility of a cyber catastrophe that would cause losses on a scale rivaling a mass disaster or pandemic. As past events on the international stage have demonstrated,[4] the Internet's structure makes it possible to attack thousands of businesses simultaneously. This specter of potentially catastrophic losses across many businesses and industries makes it harder for insurers to offer broad coverage.[5]

Because of the importance of cyber-insurance, the problems of affordability and availability, combined with the risk of correlated catastrophic losses, may make this a market where a government role is necessary, as is the case currently with terrorism, flood, and some other risks. This is certain to be much discussed in future years.[6]

11.3 Risk classification: discriminating or discriminatory?

To conduct their business, insurers must make distinctions among insureds based on how much risk they present. The price charged and amount of coverage offered is a function of this individual assessment. In addition, insurers' management of their risk pools is a process of division, where insurers offer lower premiums to those with lower risk and, at the other end of the spectrum, charge more to those with higher risk—or perhaps exclude them from the pool altogether. Insurers compete with each other by identifying lower-risk insureds to whom a lower premium can be charged; if one insurer can identify a lower-risk subset of a category of potential insureds and offer those in that subset a lower premium, the insurer may be able to attract this cohort away from other insurers who

---

4 *See* NICOLE PERLROTH, THIS IS HOW THEY TELL ME THE WORLD ENDS: THE CYBERWEAPONS ARMS RACE (2021).

5 For more discussion, *see* Kenneth S. Abraham & Daniel Schwarcz, *Courting Disaster: The Underappreciated Risk of a Cyber Insurance Catastrophe*, 27 CONN. INS. L. J. 407 (2021).

6 *See* US Gov't Accountability Office, *Cyber Insurance: Action Needed to Assess Potential Federal Response to Catastrophic Attacks*, GAO-22-104256 (June 2022), https://www.gao.gov/products/gao-22-104256.

have not yet identified the basis for making this distinction. Also, insurers charge higher-risk insureds more to combat the effects of adverse selection and moral hazard (two economic principles that were discussed in Chapter 2). Thus, insurance, by its nature, is "discriminating," but if the basis on which a distinction is drawn among potential insureds is unfair in the sense that it is widely perceived as violating a societal norm, the distinction—even if it is actuarially sound—may be deemed unlawful under the logic that it is "discriminatory."

Thus, underwriting distinctions based on race, national origin, or religion, even if these characteristics correlate with risk, are widely viewed as repugnant and therefore impermissible factors upon which to make distinctions in insurance pricing and coverage. Interestingly, underwriting distinctions based on gender have been controversial, but have not sparked a similar vigor of condemnation as have distinctions based on race, for example. In most jurisdictions in the US and until recently in Europe, it has been lawful to use gender as a factor on which to base the price of life insurance, annuities, disability insurance, health insurance (for group plans in the US), and even automobile insurance. In these products, the insured's gender correlates with the likelihood of loss. For example, women on average live longer than men, making life insurance less expensive and annuities more expensive. Young men have more auto accidents than young women, but older women on average have more auto accidents than older men. In auto insurance, gender does not *cause* loss, but it *correlates* with loss, and thus insurers can make effective use of it to distinguish between higher- and lower-risk policyholders.

Demonstrating that gender correlates with loss, however, does not demonstrate that it is fair to use it as a basis for classifying insureds. In other words, the question is whether gender should be placed in the same category as race, national origin, and religion, and deemed an impermissible rating factor. First, the number of people identifying as non-binary is significant and increasing, which calls into question the fairness of asking all applicants to identify as either male or female.[7] Second, as noted above,

---

7 In the US, as of 2022, a growing number of states have enacted statutes allowing applicants for drivers licenses to state "X" as one's gender in lieu of "M" or "F." Insurers have not responded consistently to these changes. For more discussion, *see* Michael Evans, *Do You Have to Identify as Male or Female When Getting Car Insurance?*, THE BALANCE (May 16, 2022),

gender does not *cause* auto accidents; driving habits do. Thus, it is fairer to base rates on a combination of factors that (a) directly reflect driving behaviors, such as past accident history, traffic tickets, and real-time telemetry showing how the vehicle is operated, and (b) correlate with loss and can be controlled by insureds, such as number of miles driven and geography. Third, as a general proposition, it is fairer to base risk classifications on factors insureds can control as opposed to immutable factors that insureds cannot control (e.g., race, ethnicity, gender, genetics). (People cannot control their ages, so does that mean that age cannot be used to price life insurance? As a practical matter, prohibiting the use of age in the pricing of life insurance would destroy the market.[8] As a fairness matter, it is arguably just to use age because all people "move through the ages" equally.)

How one answers the "what is fair" question depends significantly on cultural norms—the shared expectations and beliefs that shape the practices of people within social groups. In some cultures, a strong norm is that people pay for what they choose to consume; high-risk people consume more insurance and therefore should pay higher prices. Also, the norm that people should be treated "equally" is violated when high-risk people pay the same for insurance as low-risk people. Yet in health insurance, the "equal premium for equal risk" norm leads to a system where the sick and elderly pay more—and have less (or even no) coverage when premiums become too high. Excessively high premiums become a barrier to securing needed health care services, which arguably violates another norm—all people, without regard to ability to pay, should receive necessary health care services.

In other cultures, communitarianism is a much stronger norm, and this norm places limits on insurers' ability to engage in risk classification. The underlying premise in these cultures is that society should be structured in a way that risks are distributed as widely as possible across all members,

---

https://www.thebalance.com/do-you-have-to-identify-as-male-or-female-when-getting-car-insurance-5078356.

8 Charging the young and old the same for life insurance would, under the principle of adverse selection, result in a disproportionate number of older persons entering the pool—which would require price increases (or coverage decreases) to compensate for the greater risk in the pool. As prices rise, the young, seeing less value for their purchase, would drop out of the pool, which in turn would lead to a need for further price increases.

to the end that those with greater needs (in this case, risks) are supported by those with greater resources. Most agree that communitarian norms have historically been stronger in Europe than the US, where individual autonomy is highly valued and broadly distributive policies are more difficult to enact.

The question of fairness in risk classification has other dimensions as well. Insurers, in their quest for cost-effective ways to make distinctions among the members of their risk pools, have since the 1990s used consumer credit information to decide whether to offer property and casualty insurance to applicants and to set the premiums. From the perspective of the insurers who use these scores, credit history accurately predicts the frequency of insurance claims. Credit history does not cause loss, but insurers contend that the personal characteristics that generate responsible financial behaviors are the same ones that produce safe driving habits and prudent risk-reducing behaviors at home. From the perspective of those who advocate for insureds, errors in credit information are common and difficult to correct. In addition, credit information is sometimes negative because of events beyond an insured's control that have nothing to do with the insured risk—such as the insured having unexpectedly large uninsured medical bills or becoming unemployed because of a business decision made by the insured's employer. Further, critics of credit scores point to their systemic discrimination against minorities and other historically disadvantaged groups, which puts in play the discriminatory classification factors addressed earlier.

In short, what is "fair" in risk classification is a complex question on which consensus is frequently unattainable. What involves legitimate "discriminating" from one person's viewpoint may constitute unlawfully "discriminatory" classification from someone else's. At the micro level, insurance enables individuals to achieve security in the face of risk; at the macro level, insurance transfers wealth from certain segments of society to others. It is inevitable that the limits of permissible classification of risks will be vigorously debated for many years to come, but this is how it should be; what is at stake are fundamental questions about the meaning of equality, civil rights, and human dignity.[9]

---

[9] For more discussion, *see* Kenneth S. Abraham & Pierre-André Chiappori, *Classification Risk and its Regulation*, in RESEARCH HANDBOOK ON THE ECONOMICS OF INSURANCE LAW (D. Schwarcz & P. Siegelman, eds.),

11.4 Insurance and motor vehicles

One of the world's most transformative developments since 1900 is the widespread ownership of motor vehicles, primarily automobiles. No other product that is so dangerous is used by so many people, making the question of how to compensate those injured in auto accidents a matter of great consequence. In the EU and the US, the accident compensation system relies upon the tort-liability insurance apparatus as the primary pillar for compensating loss, and those who own a motor vehicle must demonstrate financial responsibility—almost universally through the purchase of liability insurance—as a prerequisite to vehicle registration, which in turn is necessary to lawfully operate a vehicle on public roads.[10] The liability system does not address, however, how someone is compensated when they injure themselves while operating a vehicle. For these losses, owners can purchase optional first-party coverages for medical expenses, lost income, and vehicle damage as part of their automobile policy. In addition, any health or disability insurance that an individual possesses will help reimburse first-party losses.

A significant weakness of the tort-liability insurance system is that it does not work when someone is injured by an uninsured motorist or an unidentified driver (i.e., a "hit-and-run" motorist). To address this gap, in the US, insureds have the option to add uninsured motorist coverage to their liability policies, which is essentially a form of first-party insurance that pays proceeds equal to what the negligent or unidentified driver would pay if that party were covered by liability insurance. In most European nations, those injured by uninsured motorists obtain compensation from a fund established by the government and financed by insurers.

Another weakness of the liability system is transactions costs. The injured person's right to proceeds depends upon establishing another person's

---

pp. 290–320 (2015); Valarie K. Blake, *Ensuring an Underclass: Stigma in Insurance*, 41 Cardozo L. Rev. 1441 (2020); Daniel Schwarcz, *Towards a Civil Rights Approach to Insurance Anti-Discrimination Law*, 69 DePaul L. Rev. 659 (2020); Jerry & Richmond, pp. 102–114.

10 For the US, see Ins. Inf. Inst., *Background on: Compulsory Auto/Uninsured Motorists* (Mar. 25, 2021), https://www.iii.org/article/background-on-compulsory-auto-uninsured-motorists. For the EU, *see* Dir. 2009/103/EC, 16 Sept. 2009, https://eur-lex.europa.eu/legal-content/EN/TXT/?uri=CELEX:32009L0103&qid=1430383119226.

fault and that person having liability insurance. If fault is contested, which is more likely with high-value losses, litigation may be necessary to resolve the claim, and this involves significant costs. Some jurisdictions in the US have experimented with no-fault systems for bodily injury claims arising out of motor vehicle accidents, reasoning that compensation can be delivered to victims more quickly if awarded without regard to fault. Personal injury lawyers have consistently, and sometimes successfully, lobbied against no-fault proposals. In some states where no-fault was enacted, legislators could not resist giving insureds more benefits than could be supported by the savings generated by the no-fault system, which then caused premiums to increase beyond what would have occurred if no-fault had not been adopted—which in turn led to public dissatisfaction with no-fault. Also, in some states, the no-fault systems have been exploited through fraud, including staged accidents and fake billings. Thus, support for no-fault in the US has ebbed, and some states have repealed their no-fault statutes and restored the liability systems.[11]

In the twenty-first century, the nature of automotive risk is undergoing profound change, and this has major ramifications for automobile insurance. Autonomous vehicles—popularly referred to as self-driving cars—are already in use throughout the world, usually in pilot programs. Although there are currently various levels of automation that require distinct levels of human involvement to operate such vehicles, the technology is changing rapidly. Fully autonomous vehicles may be commercially available by the 2030s; some observers predict that they will be safe, reliable, affordable, and in widespread use in the 2040s or 2050s.[12] According to some estimates, autonomous vehicles may eliminate driver error completely. On the one hand, this is good because autonomous automobiles may eliminate 80 to 90 percent of all accidents. On the other hand, eliminating driver error as a factor in motor vehicle accidents changes the premise—the liability of the vehicle operator—on which the

---

11 For more discussion of auto insurance in the US, including no fault systems, *see* JERRY & RICHMOND, pp. 805–856. For more discussion of auto insurance in the EU, *see* European Commission, *Motor Insurance* (undated), https://finance.ec.europa.eu/insurance-and-pension-funds/insurance/motor-insurance_en.

12 For more on the future of autonomous vehicles, *see* Todd Litman, *Autonomous Vehicle Implementation Predictions*, Victoria Transport Pol'y Inst. (November 6, 2022), www.vtpi.org/avip.docx.

modern compensation system is based. This will require rethinking how compensation is structured for victims in the accidents that do occur.

In any compensation system based on liability, evolution in the nature of the liability risk inevitably leads to evolution of the liability insurance product. Thus, as the driver is removed from the equation as the cause of automobile accidents, it is likely that fault in accidents will shift to vehicle manufacturers and the manufacturers of the software that controls them. In other words, products liability will become the organizing principle under which auto accident victim compensation is provided, and automobile insurance will likely evolve into a category of product liability insurance sold to manufacturers.[13] Cyber-insurance will be relevant, too; the automated operation systems will be at risk for hacking, perhaps systemically. Also, for many years, traditional driver-operated vehicles will coexist on the highways with autonomous vehicles, which will complicate underwriting and pricing. Eventually, it may be that the automobile insurance industry as it now exists will become obsolete—like other industries that have confronted disruptive technologies. The implications are profound; automobile insurance, by itself, accounts for more than one-third of all premium dollars in the property and casualty insurance industry,[14] which is another way of saying that autonomous vehicles will cause transformative shifts in products, underwriting, and pricing.

---

13 For more discussion, *see* Kenneth S. Abraham & Robert L. Rabin, *Automated Vehicles and Manufacturer Responsibility for Accidents: A New Legal Regime for a New Era*, 105 Va. L. Rev. 127 (2019); Daniel A. Crane, Kyle D. Logue & Bryce C. Pilz, *A Survey of Legal Issues Arising from the Deployment of Autonomous and Connected Vehicles,* 23 Mich. Telecom. & Tech. L. Rev. 191 (2017).

14 In 2021, 42.4 percent of all property and casualty premiums written in the US were for private passenger and commercial auto insurance (a sector which employed approximately 627,000 people and had net premiums of about USD 700 billion). Ins. Inf. Inst., *Insurance Facts* (undated), https://www.iii.org/publications/triple-i-insurance-facts/property-casualty-insurance-by-line/auto/premiums (citing NAIC data sourced from S&P Global Market Intelligence).

11.5 Insurance, order, and social regulation

David Easton famously defined politics as the "authoritative allocation of values for society."[15] Usually, allocating values is understood as something governments do as part of the political process, but the reality is that values are allocated when insurance companies conduct their business. Chapter 6 discussed how insurance policies are often structured to influence policyholder behavior; deductibles and coinsurance cause policyholders to share financial responsibility for losses, which incentivizes insureds to take precautions to avoid loss. The same incentives exist when insurers charge policyholders more premium if they engage in risk-increasing behaviors. Of course, if a policyholder finds more utility in continuing to engage in a risky behavior than the disutility suffered from the increased cost of insuring it, the behavior will continue, but at least the higher premium requires the policyholder to internalize the cost of taking more risks. In short, when private insurance companies make decisions about premiums, deductibles, coinsurance requirements, and policy limits, embedded in many of those decisions are statements about desired policyholder behaviors and internalizations of costs.

Chapter 2 discussed roles of insurance beyond risk spreading, and one of those was influencing social norms. Whether insurers, as private entities, have intentions about public values is debatable (they presumably do when the substance of a public norm impacts how they conduct their business), but the decisions of insurers, whatever their purposes may be, operate functionally as allocations of social values. When insurers decide what rating factors they will use to price insurance (and when government regulators approve or disapprove these decisions), the regulation of policyholder behavior and the approval (or disapproval) of certain values are obvious. Some choices are, of course, more controversial than others, but each decision makes a statement about how society should be organized and how people should behave, which is the essence of governance and the authoritative allocation of values. For example, increasing auto insurance premiums for accident-prone individuals seeks to induce these persons to drive more carefully. Increasing premiums to the owners of high-rise buildings who do not perform routine inspections of structural integrity or who fail to make needed repairs promptly seeks to encourage

---

15 David Easton, A Framework for Political Analysis (1965), p. 50.

responsible behaviors. Insurers encourage specific behaviors when they reduce premiums for homeowners who install smoke detectors, burglar alarms, or hurricane-resistant roofs and windows (if they live on a coast susceptible to hurricanes), or who raise the elevation of their homes (if they live in a flood zone), or who do not own bite-prone dogs as pets or purchase trampolines for children's play. Insurers also encourage specific behaviors if they refuse to insure homes with unfenced swimming pools or precarious tree limbs hanging over them. These pricing policies require insureds who choose to engage in higher-risk activities to internalize the cost of that risk (think of this as imposing a tax on those insureds), and this in turn deters some individuals from choosing to pursue these behaviors. Thus, people choose insurance to shed risk and achieve certainty in the face of insecurity, but insurance also shapes the choices people make in daily life.[16]

This conjures up the notion that insurance serves purposes broader than securing protection from the risk of adverse events. Insurance can be understood as a form of social responsibility—where the well-off participate in pools to help those with greater needs (a kind of communitarianism), and where certain behaviors are expected of those admitted to the pool for the protection of the common good. Those who do not adhere to these expectations are removed from the pool or are required to pay more to avoid a forced exit. The extent to which contra-communitarian behaviors are tolerated makes statements about—and reflects a governance decision on—the importance of individual freedom and self-autonomy. Kenneth Abraham calls this, quite appropriately, a kind of "surrogate government"—that "[g]overnment in effect relies on insurers to perform some functions that government could legitimately perform but does not."[17]

When government enters the picture in its role as the regulator of insurance entities, its determinations become the statements about desired behaviors and internalizations of costs. In other words, as discussed in Chapter 2, when government requires insurers to provide designated coverages in their policies (or prohibits certain coverages), regulates pricing,

---

16 *See* Tom Baker & Rick Swedloff, *Regulation by Liability Insurance: From Auto to Lawyers Professional Responsibility*, 60 UCLA L. Rev. 1412 (2013).

17 Kenneth S. Abraham, *Four Conceptions of Insurance*, 161 U. Pa. L. Rev. 653, 685 (2013).

or mandates the purchase of insurance by individuals or businesses, insurance becomes a tool government uses to influence the allocation of social values that reside outside insurance's risk transfer and distribution function.

To illustrate, consider the prevalence of gun ownership in the US, where gun homicide is as much as 26 times and gun suicide is nearly 12 times higher than in other high-income nations,[18] and controversy about what to do about this, if anything, is intense. What would happen if government were to require gun owners to purchase liability insurance for the consequences of the use of their weapons? First, it would raise the cost of gun ownership, which at the margin would deter some people from owning guns—or owning as many as they do. If a demonstration of insurance coverage were required to purchase a firearm, fewer purchases would occur (especially by young buyers with a history of mental illness or violent behavior for whom insurers would be expected to price the insurance at multiple times the price of a gun). Second, if insurers were allowed to price the coverage based on the amount of risk presented by individual insureds, insurers would reduce premiums for those who demonstrate their adherence to gun safety practices. If premium reductions were offered to those who own gun safes, use firearm safety locks, acquire smart-gun technology that allows guns to be fired only by their owners, and complete gun safety training, these accident-reducing behaviors would be encouraged—with a consequent reduction in accidents, suicides, and thefts of guns by criminals (and their use). If an insured's premiums increase in the future due to the negligent failure to secure a firearm resulting in a thief using the gun to commit a crime, insureds will pay more attention to their storage practices today—just like the prospect of increased auto insurance premiums for future accidents encourages safe driving behaviors today. Criminals and mass shooters are unlikely to be deterred by insurance premiums, but the net effect of a liability insurance requirement would be to change some gun ownership behaviors by some policyholders.

Another issue where insurance regulation is inextricably linked to social values is abortion. Soon after the US Supreme Court's 1973 decision in

---

18 *See* BBC News, *Mass Shootings: America's Challenge for Gun Control Explained in Seven Charts* (October 12, 2022), https://www.bbc.com/news/world-us-canada-41488081.

Roe v. Wade,[19] where the Court held that the US Constitution protects a woman's right to an abortion prior to the viability of the fetus, efforts began at the state and federal level to limit insurance coverage for abortion. In 1977, Congress banned federal funding for abortion, with some exceptions, which had the effect of removing federal support for abortions under the Medicaid health insurance program. In the ensuing years, many states enacted restrictions on the use of state funds to support Medicaid abortions, thereby greatly constricting access to abortion for Medicaid recipients. Many states also limited private plans' coverage of abortion and banned abortion coverage in plans offered through the 2010 Affordable Care Act's marketplace. In contrast to those states that used coverage restrictions and bans to implement anti-abortion policies, a number of states placed no limitations on coverage and some others affirmatively required both group and individual plans to include abortion coverage, thereby implementing pro-women's reproductive rights policies.[20]

Insurance also plays a role in another important social value—how resources are distributed within society. As discussed in Chapter 2, whenever government requires the use of a rating factor that departs from actuarial fairness, assets are redistributed from one group to another. Health insurance (as explained in Chapter 2) is a powerful illustration of this phenomenon, but the same redistributive process is operative for any insurance product where government intervenes in the market for public purposes. Redistribution occurs because whenever a lower-risk group is required to pay a higher premium than actuarial fairness requires, this group will spend assets they could have spent on other things of value to them. For the same reason, the higher-risk group would have had fewer discretionary assets at their disposal if they had paid the actuarially fair price for insurance, but the subsidy this cohort receives enables them to

---

19 410 U.S. 113 (1973). *Roe* was overturned by the Court's decision in *Dobbs v. Jackson Women's Health Organization*, 597 U.S. ---, 2022 WL 2276808 (June 24, 2022). *Dobbs* does not change the dynamic through which states can use insurance regulation to promote state policies on abortion and women's reproductive freedom. In states that now choose to criminalize abortion, insurance coverage is almost certain to be prohibited.

20 For more discussion, *see* Kaiser Family Foundation, *Interactive: How State Policies Shape Access to Abortion Coverage* (May 12, 2022), https://www.kff.org/womens-health-policy/issue-brief/interactive-how-state-policies-shape-access-to-abortion-coverage/.

accumulate extra discretionary assets—at the expense of the lower-risk cohort. In short, when government regulates insurer risk classification, it engages in a process of asset redistribution, with all the social implications that this reallocation entails.

Spencer Kimball observed over sixty years ago that insurance reflects the purposes of the larger world outside it.[21] This is certainly true, but insurance does more than this. François Ewald more recently wrote that "[t]he values associated with insurance have … a political dimension. They are the result of societal choice."[22] Insurance is not merely reflective; it is instrumental. Insurance serves powerful risk-management functions, and in that application has the potential to help solve pressing problems facing humankind. But insurance also shapes—and can be used deliberately and proactively to shape—the values of the world in which we live.

---

21 Spencer Kimball, *The Purpose of Insurance Regulation: A Preliminary Inquiry in the Theory of Insurance Law*, 45 Minn. L. Rev. 471, 524 (1961).

22 François Ewald, *The Values of Insurance*, 74 Grey Room 120, 140 (Mar. 1, 2019) (trans. Shana Cooperstein & Benjamin Young).

Index

Titles in the **Elgar Advanced Introductions** series include:

International Political Economy
Benjamin J. Cohen

The Austrian School of Economics
Randall G. Holcombe

Cultural Economics
Ruth Towse

Law and Development
Michael J. Trebilcock and Mariana Mota Prado

International Humanitarian Law
Robert Kolb

International Trade Law
Michael J. Trebilcock

Post Keynesian Economics
J.E. King

International Intellectual Property
Susy Frankel and Daniel J. Gervais

Public Management and Administration
Christopher Pollitt

Organised Crime
Leslie Holmes

Nationalism
Liah Greenfeld

Social Policy
Daniel Béland and Rianne Mahon

Globalisation
Jonathan Michie

Entrepreneurial Finance
Hans Landström

International Conflict and Security Law
Nigel D. White

Comparative Constitutional Law
Mark Tushnet

International Human Rights Law
Dinah L. Shelton

Entrepreneurship
Robert D. Hisrich

International Tax Law
Reuven S. Avi-Yonah

Public Policy
B. Guy Peters

The Law of International Organizations
Jan Klabbers

International Environmental Law
Ellen Hey

International Sales Law
Clayton P. Gillette

Corporate Venturing
Robert D. Hisrich

Public Choice
Randall G. Holcombe

Private Law
Jan M. Smits

Consumer Behavior Analysis
Gordon Foxall

Behavioral Economics
John F. Tomer

Cost–Benefit Analysis
Robert J. Brent

Environmental Impact Assessment
Angus Morrison-Saunders

Comparative Constitutional Law, Second Edition
Mark Tushnet

National Innovation Systems
Cristina Chaminade, Bengt-Åke Lundvall and Shagufta Haneef

Ecological Economics
Matthias Ruth

Private International Law and Procedure
Peter Hay

Freedom of Expression
Mark Tushnet

Law and Globalisation
Jaakko Husa

Regional Innovation Systems
Bjørn T. Asheim, Arne Isaksen and Michaela Trippl

International Political Economy Second Edition
Benjamin J. Cohen

International Tax Law Second Edition
Reuven S. Avi-Yonah

Social Innovation
Frank Moulaert and Diana MacCallum

The Creative City
Charles Landry

International Trade Law
Michael J. Trebilcock and Joel Trachtman

European Union Law
Jacques Ziller

Planning Theory
Robert A. Beauregard

Tourism Destination Management
Chris Ryan

International Investment Law
August Reinisch

Sustainable Tourism
David Weaver

Austrian School of Economics Second Edition
Randall G. Holcombe

U.S. Criminal Procedure
Christopher Slobogin

Platform Economics
Robin Mansell and W. Edward Steinmueller

Public Finance
Vito Tanzi

Feminist Economics
Joyce P. Jacobsen

Human Dignity and Law
James R. May and Erin Daly

Space Law
Frans G. von der Dunk

National Accounting
John M. Hartwick

Legal Research Methods
Ernst Hirsch Ballin

Privacy Law
Megan Richardson

International Human Rights Law
Second Edition
Dinah L. Shelton

Law and Artificial Intelligence
Woodrow Barfield and Ugo Pagallo

Politics of International Human Rights
David P. Forsythe

Community-based Conservation
Fikret Berkes

Global Production Networks
Neil M. Coe

Mental Health Law
Michael L. Perlin

Law and Literature
Peter Goodrich

Creative Industries
John Hartley

Global Administration Law
Sabino Cassese

Housing Studies
William A.V. Clark

Global Sports Law
Stephen F. Ross

Public Policy
B. Guy Peters

Empirical Legal Research
Herbert M. Kritzer

Cities
Peter J. Taylor

Law and Entrepreneurship
Shubha Ghosh

Mobilities
Mimi Sheller

Technology Policy
Albert N. Link and James Cunningham

Urban Transport Planning
Kevin J. Krizek and David A. King

Legal Reasoning
Larry Alexander and Emily Sherwin

Sustainable Competitive Advantage in Sales
Lawrence B. Chonko

Law and Development
Second Edition
Mariana Mota Prado and Michael J. Trebilcock

Law and Renewable Energy
Joel B. Eisen

Experience Economy
Jon Sundbo

Marxism and Human Geography
Kevin R. Cox

Maritime Law
Paul Todd

American Foreign Policy
Loch K. Johnson

Water Politics
Ken Conca

Business Ethics
John Hooker

Employee Engagement
Alan M. Saks and Jamie A. Gruman

Governance
Jon Pierre and B. Guy Peters

Demography
Wolfgang Lutz

Environmental Compliance and Enforcement
LeRoy C. Paddock

Migration Studies
Ronald Skeldon

Landmark Criminal Cases
George P. Fletcher

Comparative Legal Methods
Pier Giuseppe Monateri

U.S. Environmental Law
E. Donald Elliott and Daniel C. Esty

Gentrification
Chris Hamnett

Family Policy
Chiara Saraceno

Law and Psychology
Tom R. Tyler

Advertising
Patrick De Pelsmacker

New Institutional Economics
Claude Ménard and Mary M. Shirley

The Sociology of Sport
Eric Anderson and Rory Magrath

The Sociology of Peace Processes
John D. Brewer

Social Protection
James Midgley

Corporate Finance
James A. Brickley and Clifford W. Smith Jr

U.S. Federal Securities Law
Thomas Lee Hazen

Cybersecurity Law
David P. Fidler

The Sociology of Work
Amy S. Wharton

Marketing Strategy
George S. Day

Scenario Planning
Paul Schoemaker

Financial Inclusion
Robert Lensink, Calumn Hamilton and Charles Adjasi

Children's Rights
Wouter Vandenhole and Gamze Erdem Türkelli

Sustainable Careers
Jeffrey H. Greenhaus and Gerard A. Callanan

Business and Human Rights
Peter T. Muchlinski

Spatial Statistics
Daniel A. Griffith and Bin Li

The Sociology of the Self
Shanyang Zhao

Artificial Intelligence in Healthcare
Tom Davenport, John Glaser and Elizabeth Gardner

Central Banks and Monetary Policy
Jakob de Haan and Christiaan Pattipeilohy

Megaprojects
Nathalie Drouin and Rodney Turner

Social Capital
Karen S. Cook

Elections and Voting
Ian McAllister

Negotiation
Leigh Thompson and Cynthia S. Wang

Youth Studies
Howard Williamson and James E. Côté

Private Equity
Paul A. Gompers and Steven N. Kaplan

Digital Marketing
Utpal Dholakia

Water Economics and Policy
Ariel Dinar

Disaster Risk Reduction
Douglas Paton

Social Movements and Political Protests
Karl-Dieter Opp

Radical Innovation
Joe Tidd

Pricing Strategy and Analytics
Vithala R. Rao

Bounded Rationality
Clement A. Tisdell

International Food Law
Neal D. Fortin

International Conflict and Security Law
Second Edition
Nigel D. White

Entrepreneurial Finance
Second Edition
Hans Landström

US Civil Liberties
Susan N. Herman

Resilience
Fikret Berkes

Insurance Law
Robert H. Jerry, II